A DREAM COME TRUE

Simple Techniques for Dream Interpretation and Precognitive Dream Recognition

Susan,

Dreams have much to tell those who are willing to listen. May your dreams show you what you need to see,

A DREAM COME TRUE

Simple Techniques for Dream Interpretation
and Precognitive Dream Recognition

BY DAVID L. KAHN

COSIMO

NEW YORK

"If you find yourself having dreams about being chased or fighting something, make a conscious decision next time to stop running and stop fighting. Turn around and face whatever 'it' is. This sounds hard to do. How can you love some hideous-looking creature that you perceive is trying to hurt you? You must remember that this is merely a physical representation of your fears and anxieties. Do not fear these dreams. They are opportunities to heal yourself, and to rid yourself of harmful habits. Show your monster love."

——from *A Dream Come True*

A DREAM
COME TRUE

Simple Techniques for Dream Interpretation
and Precognitive Dream Recognition

BY DAVID L. KAHN

International Association for the Study of Dreams (IASD)
asdreams.org

The World Dreams Peace Bridge
worlddreamspeacebridge.org

The Lucid Dream Exchange
dreaminglucid.com

lucid.reverie@yahoo.com

On the eve of the March 2003 attack on Iraq, members of the international online group the World Dreams Peace Bridge dreamed together for world peace. Many members of the group dreamed about the children of Iraq. Out of these dreams grew the Aid for Traumatized Children Project, an action directed toward providing support and relief for the many thousands of children displaced, injured, traumatized, and suffering as a result of this war.

The Aid for Traumatized Children Project has brought together people from many countries, including Iraq, to discuss what can be done for the children. It has provided aid for Seasons Art School in Baghdad, for the Post Traumatic Stress Program of Dr. Ali Rashed in the Middle East, and for refugee children in Jordan. The program continues to gain support as people reach out to help.

David L. Kahn, author of this book, says, "I found my way to the World Dreams Peace Bridge through a series of synchronistic events. Immediately I felt a sense of belonging with the other members, and I was drawn to the Aid for Traumatized Children Project. I feel strongly that we all have a responsibility to the children of the world, regardless of what country they live in, or what the politics or religion of that country are. For this reason, I have chosen to donate the royalties of this book to the AFTC. I invite you to join me in contributing to this important cause."

The Aid for Traumatized Children Project exists under the umbrella of the iMAGE Project, a 501(c)3 educational nonprofit organization. Donations to the AFTC Project can be made online at worlddreamspeacebridge.org or to the iMAGE Project at 408 Elmhurst Lane, Portsmouth, VA 23701. Please indicate "AFTC Project" in the memo area.

Table of Contents

Acknowledgements

A heartfelt thank you goes out to everyone who has supported me, encouraged me, and assisted me.

To my wife, Chris, thank you for never allowing me to doubt myself and for believing that I have something worthwhile to contribute to the world. To my children—Jacob, Amanda, Heather, and Kristin—you are, every day, the reason that I strive to be the best man that I can be. Mom and Dad, thank you for raising me to be a freethinker and for always being there for me, no matter what. To my brother, Bruce; all of my friends; and my extended family: I thank every one of you. I'm very lucky to be surrounded by the people that I am surrounded by.

A very special thank you goes out to the members of the International Association for the Study of Dreams, the World Peace Dreams Bridge, and the Lucid Dream Exchange. In particular I would like to recognize Jean Campbell, whose work is the foundation for my support of the Aid for Traumatized Children. Others whom I would like to thank for their assistance, advice, and guidance include Gloria Sturzenacker, Liz Diaz, Sheila Asato, Robert Waggoner, Lucy Gillis, Patricia Garfield, and Wendy Pannier.

To any child who suffers from the consequences of war, poverty, disease, and persecution, you are not forgotten.

Foreword

by Jean Campbell, President, 2006–7,
The International Association for the Study of Dreams

There are a few times in my life when I have read a book about dream work and said to myself at the end of it, "He really nailed it. What a good job!" That was my response to David L. Kahn's *A Dream Come True.*

Why is this such a good book?

For people who have not worked with their dreams before, David introduces a method that brings immediate, verifiable results—not from another person, not from an "expert"...but from the dreamer.

In his attempt to teach himself how to find the meaning in his dreams, David developed a technique for dream interpretations that only asks us to try.

What's more, he noticed while doing his personal dream study that his dreams, and the dreams of others he knew, seemed to contain elements of precognition, or that they pointed to a future that eventually appeared in waking reality. Having discovered this, he set out to tell the story of what worked for him, and to explain his method so others could try it too.

A personable and delightful account of one man working through the messages contained in his dreams, *A Dream Come True* leads us through the process to successes of our own.

I first met David as he was following his dreams. "Following the bread crumbs" is what he called it in an e-mail he sent to the World Dreams Peace Bridge. David first followed his dreams to the International Association for the Study of Dreams in September 2006, where he discovered that the current IASD board chair, Harvard professor David Kahn, shared both his name and his interest in dreams. It was a clue.

When he enrolled in IASD's annual PsiberDreaming online conference, David found a world of other dreamers from around the globe, including several who are members of the World Dreams Peace Bridge. He was immediately attracted to the Peace Bridge as a group that shares not only his interest in dreams but his interest in helping the hundreds of thousands of children displaced by the ongoing war in Iraq. Without further invitation, David announced to me that he wanted to donate the proceeds of this book to the Aid for Traumatized Children Project, the part of the Peace Bridge that has raised funds for Iraqi children since a series of shared dreams in March 2003.

David has been following his dreams for many years now, as he recounts in *A Dream Come True*. The information in these pages is your invitation to do the same. I am honored and pleased to be part of this publishing event.

I hear the whispers

Show me…
The way

Lead me…
Home

Tell me…
Shall I whisper back?

Living the life of your dreams

The ocean was blue a moment ago
Its image now sharpened to indigo
Red's become crimson, the sky midnight
The stars now shine a more radiant light

The air is felt as wind on my skin
I see where I'm going and know where I've been
There's always a guide to show me the way
But maybe I should escort today

When you learn how to interpret your dreams, it is like having a therapist with you at all times who knows everything about you. Your dreams always tell you what you need to know in order to help you find peace and happiness. I'm not suggesting that you quit seeing your therapist, but dreams bluntly tell you whatever it is that you need to know, tailored specifically for you.

When you know that you interpret a dream correctly, it can be an exhilarating feeling. Often people think that they know what their dreams are about, but when you nail it, the feelings are much more intense. It is like taking a test and knowing that you got the answers right without having to see your score, or like taking a shot at a basketball hoop and knowing that the ball is going in after it leaves your hand. You just know it. You nailed it.

As you learn to interpret your dreams, you will see that the messages are often simple but powerful. Some of the lessons that I have learned from my dreams include the following:

Get outside and walk. This will calm my mind.

Getting a second job right now is not a good idea.

I am ready to get married.

We won't have a lot of financial security, but it will be enough.

It is okay for me to allow my daughters to have more independence.

Allow others to make their own mistakes.

Even if people don't respond, they often still receive the message.

Being kind and patient is more important than being right.

I need to eat a healthier diet.

Whenever I know that I have properly interpreted a dream, it fills me with positive feelings, both because of the knowledge that I got it right and because I understand what it is that my higher self is trying to say to me. Those positive feelings can last for hours or days, and some of the lessons that I have learned have changed my entire outlook on life. I bet you would be hard pressed to find a person who knows how to interpret their dreams who does not make peace and a sense of spirituality an important aspect of their life. The better you get at interpreting your dreams, the more mysterious they become. "Dreamers" tend to be very spiritual people whose lives are filled with "coincidences" as described in Chapter 2 and throughout this book.

The good news for you is that this tool to create a better life is absolutely free. Your age, race, gender, religion, or other labels do not affect your ability to be successful. You do not need a degree, and in fact someone with a more analytical mind may actually have a more difficult time even recalling their dreams, much less interpreting them.

I won't say too much about dream recall. If you are looking to interpret your dreams, I will assume that you probably already remember at least some of them and that you are looking to figure out what they mean. If not, there are many good books available to help you with dream recall. There are a few ideas that do work well for dream recall as well as dream interpretation, and I will briefly discuss those. One is that it is a good idea to keep a pad and paper by the bed. Jot down what you remember when you wake up. You do not need to write out the whole dream at that time, but just some words or notes that will help you recall it later. That is effective for me. I keep a book light on my pad so that I can jot down words in the middle of the night. Later in the day when I have time, I type my dreams in my computer. I date and title each dream. Dating them helps me see patterns during a block of time. The same people, places, objects, or events may show up in several dreams. The title helps me quickly remember what the dream was. Often by simply viewing the title, I can recall the whole dream. It makes it easier to sort through them later.

When I type out my dreams in my computer, I use the present tense rather than "I recall" or "I remember." I use phrases like "I see…" or "I am driving…" I have found this to help in making connections between my actions in dreams and actions in waking life. The last thing I will mention on the subject of writing down dreams is that you should be detailed. Everything has a meaning. What color is the carpet? Is it light or dark in the room? What is the weather like? What direction are you driving? Are you using your right hand or left? What or who is in the background? Describe the ceiling, brick, clothing, facial structures, or anything else that you can. Are you participating in the events unfolding, or are you simply observing them? What angle are you looking at? Are you above, below, or to the side? It may be those details hiding behind the big scenes that are the key.

There are many examples of dreams in this book that I use to describe various interpretation techniques. Since dreams can be lengthy and detailed, I have edited down many of the example dreams to weed out the parts that are not related to that element of interpretation. Narrowing down a dream into smaller sections is one of the techniques that I will discuss in more detail later in Chapter 23.

Dreams are, in a manner of speaking, egotistical. You aren't dreaming about someone else's problem. You are dreaming about how that person's problem affects you. Knowing this will help you make proper interpretations. If someone else is sad or angry, the dream is about how that makes you feel. Perhaps you feel that someone else is dragging you down, or maybe his or her sadness is making you sad. Look at the dream as though it was custom made just for you, because it was.

CHAPTER 1

The whispers

Follow the whispered trail
Its path is made of stone
Share where trust has earned its right
Then leave the others alone

Judge not the judgmental troupe itself
Concrete alleys are hidden from view
Reach for one of your stones instead
And bid their perceptions adieu

Express your right for optimism
Send apathy on its way
Censor not your precedence
Lest contentment will decay

True confidence is a quiet affair
Only in spirit you can hear
'Tis your whispers arranging the stones
That you step on without fear

Words and judgments are a gift, my friend
Though a gift you need not take
Learn to master what wounds you most
And, with a whisper, you shall awake

Dreaming of the future is something very common to those who frequently recall their dreams. Figuring out what part of your dream is a premonition and what it means to you is much the same as any other dream interpretation. In fact, learning how to properly interpret your dreams is a prerequisite for being able to see a premonition when it does occur and to understand the relationship to what is occurring in your life at that moment. Much of this book is therefore dedicated to interpretation as a whole. In later chapters I will describe how my own dreams have assisted me in the process of going much further with interpretation techniques, including recognizing premonitions. I'll begin by explaining the different kinds of premonition dreams with examples so that you can understand what it is that you can expect of your own dreams after you learn the techniques in this book.

There are two different kinds of premonition dreams. The first type is one that prepares you for something that hasn't yet happened, but at some level you are aware is coming. We often push things beneath the surface of our consciousness because we aren't ready to fully deal with it. At other times, we haven't consciously realized that something is going to happen in our future, but there are clues that our subconscious is picking up on.

> *I am in a library and there are a lot of boxes stacked up three levels high. I am living in a box on the lower end. I am going to be getting a promotion.*

This is a dream that my teenage stepdaughter had some months before her mother and I got engaged. I was living in the suburbs of Minneapolis and they were living in a small town 250 miles away. I asked my stepdaughter what a box was to her. She described it as something people use to pack or move with, and that it has six sides. I recognized the description of the stacked boxes as the same shape as my apartment building—three levels high with my apartment on the lower end. Even though we had not specifically discussed the idea of them moving, I had been dating her mother for several months and it was obvious that the relationship was serious. I have joint custody of my other three children with my ex-wife and therefore I needed to remain in the same area that I was already living at. My stepdaughter's subconscious was picking up on the idea that this relationship was headed toward us all living together, and that would mean them being the ones to move. Interestingly, she had described a box as having six sides, which is the number of people now living together in our family. Fortunately, this dream also viewed it as a promotion. This is a very good example of a dream having the purpose of preparing someone for a big change in her life.

I have noticed in my own dreams that the weather is often a preparation of things to come.

> *I am standing outside of a restaurant and staring out into the sky. I see a storm coming. The clouds are dark and I can feel the wind picking up. It is going to be a bad storm, but I am calm as I watch it.*

This dream occurred as I was going through my divorce. Although I knew it was going to be a difficult process, I didn't realize just how difficult, expensive, and lengthy it would end up.

The following storm example makes a different prediction.

> *I am sitting inside of a restaurant. The lights are out, but the large front*
> *windows provide enough light. I see a sport utility vehicle drive up in*
> *front of the restaurant. My friend Mike steps out. He is wearing a nice*
> *suit. He comes up to me and warns me that a storm is coming. That*
> *is all he was there for. I knew it would rain and maybe lightning and*
> *thunder, but it didn't seem like the storm would be too bad.*

I didn't realize at first what this was about, but I found out within a couple of days. I have some arthritis. I generally do very well with it and I can go months on end with little or no symptoms, but here and there it acts up on me. I had been feeling some minor aches in the days prior to this dream. In the days following my symptoms got somewhat worse and I realized that I was having a bit of an arthritis flare-up. Again, this dream was simply preparing me for what was to come. It also let me know that it wouldn't be too bad, which it wasn't.

The other type of premonition dream is one in which the information that you receive about a future event comes from someplace other than your own mind. In these cases, you see, hear, or experience something in real life that is strikingly similar to something you had experienced in a dream prior to the event. In my case, these similarities often show up one to three days after the dream. The similarities are not always so exact that you could call it absolute evidence. I suppose you could call them "very coincidental." However, these "very coincidental" dreams happen so often that the frequency itself would also have to be labeled "very coincidental." It seems that it is quite common in people that recall and pay attention to their dreams to have premonitions about things that they could not possibly have known about in advance of the dream. More interestingly, sometimes I can interpret the dream only after the event. My feelings and emotions are tied into these dreams in the same way as other dreams, except that the event occurred *after* the dream.

> *A very large woman is standing beside me. Her belly looks like the*
> *shape of the front end of our car. She is supposedly my friend's mom,*
> *although she doesn't look like anyone that I've seen. She says, "I weigh*
> *seven thousand pounds." She repeats that very slow a few more times:*
> *"I weigh seven thousand pounds."*

Upon awakening, I couldn't figure this dream out. As I will explain in a later chapter, disproportionately large items in dreams are common, and a way in which the dream is calling your attention to it. In this case the large woman was calling my attention. But I couldn't place what it could be about. The one thing I knew is that she was really trying to get me to hear that she weighed seven thousand pounds. I told my wife that morning about this dream, and even said to her, "Don't be surprised if the number seven thousand shows up in the near future." A couple of hours later, we went to an embroidery shop. My father had asked us to check on some pricing to put our company logo on some shirts. I had never been to an embroidery shop before, so the shop owner explained the process to me. After looking at the logo and listening to how we wanted it done, he said to me, "I estimate this to be seven thousand stitches." After leaving the store, I said to my wife, "Now I know where the number seven thousand came from." She stopped walking, looked at me, and said, "I just got a chill." She's heard this kind of thing so many times since that she's no longer surprised, but the feelings of awe and bewilderment never go away.

As you can see, my example is coincidental but hardly proof. What I can tell you is that I never once had a dream that I can recall with the number seven thousand in it prior to this, or since. I can't recall the number seven thousand showing up with any meaning in my life, but on this particular day it showed up in both my dream and waking life. As coincidental as this seems, I still would brush it off if it weren't for the fact that this happens all the time. When I say all the time, I mean that for me it occurs often a few times per week or more. After a while, you get to expect it and it just becomes an odd but fun part of your life.

> *I am in a hotel room looking out of the window. The hotel either has a second building, or this one curves because I am facing part of the hotel with windows facing toward me. I see my friend Mike in a window across from me, one floor down. There are other cops with him and I see that Mike has his gun out. I also have a gun with me. I know that they are looking for a bad guy who got into the building. I look to the side and I see that a large group of women are being evacuated from the building.*

I titled this dream "Evacuation" in my journal. The following day, I received a phone call from my daughter's school. There was a bomb threat and they evacuated the school. There were a number of police officers on the scene. I ended up going to pick her up at another nearby school where the students had been brought. I had a few other cop dreams in the few days prior to this, but not after. My friend Mike had shown up in several of them. Since he is a cop, he is my first association with the profession.

Over time I have come to realize that a significant percentage of dreams, if not all of them, have some premonition substance to them. As I reviewed many of my own dreams as research for this book, it was startling to me just how often this actually occurs.

One theory that I have about the odd symbolisms in dreams is that many of the symbols have not yet showed up in your life. There is a mixture of past, present, and future in almost all dreams. The actions in the dreams are very present tense. It is what you are doing, or dealing with, right now. The location may be present tense, but is just as likely to be someplace from your past or even a mixture of both. The objects, people, or some events that you see in dreams are frequently of things that you haven't yet seen in waking life. To me, the feeling is much like déjà vu, except that I'm aware of where I had seen this before.

"The whispers" are what I have named the coincidences, synchronicities, signs, and odd occurrences that I have learned to be guides. The whispers provide me with what I need, when I need it. Sometimes they just give me a sign to let me know that I'm right where I'm supposed to be. The more dreaming becomes a part of your life, the more you will hear your own whispers.

The next several chapters will show you several easy and effective ways to interpret your dreams. If you follow the instructions and put them into practice, you will get good at interpretation. You most likely will also improve your dream recall, and your own whispers will become more frequent and recognizable. When you learn to interpret your dreams, your entire world will change. Once you have nailed one interpretation, I am certain that you will know this to be true.

CHAPTER 2

Emotions are the building blocks of dreams

Don't fear the duplicity
I'll rouse equanimity for thee
Unlock the gate of your soul
Let not angst take its toll

'Tis time to liberate your dismay
A kiss goodnight, may it slumber today
Alas, betrayal is left behind
Tonight, you may rest amidst kind

Dreams do not come from events that occur in your life. They come from how you process those events. How you think and feel in the present is what creates your dreams. Your dream may include symbolisms from yesterday, a week ago, or twenty years ago, but it is your feelings right now that are creating the dream. So, the major theme of a dream is *generally* present tense. What often happens is that some event will occur during your day and your mind will process it. It could be a comment that you hear, something that you see, or a smell that reminds you of your grandmother's cooking. That thought triggers an emotion, and the emotion shows up in your dream. However, the emotion will show up in the dream only if you need to further process it. If you feel the emotion of missing your grandmother, you probably won't dream about it unless her passing is recent or you are having difficulty with the grieving process.

4. **Notice emotions that you associate with the places and objects in your dream.**

   With my example, my childhood room was a place of security and yet I also felt locked in. I didn't necessarily want to spend my time in there, but there was nowhere else to go where I was comfortable. To help in the interpretation of this dream, I had to ask myself in what way was I locking myself up (figuratively) in order to feel more secure. I was indeed acting guarded with my emotions as a means of security.

CHAPTER 3

Viewing your dreams in 3D

> *I see him*
> *The man that is*
> *The child that was*
> *From above*
> *In front*
> *Behind*
> *But not as me*
>
> *... The ghostly observer*
> *Sees as they do*

Do you ever wonder why dreams seem to be so strange? If they have a message, why don't they just come out and say what it is? One of the main reasons is that dreams are about several things at one time. They are efficient in this way. We have so much going on in our lives that we wouldn't have enough sleep time to cover it all if dreams were only about one thing. Often dreams will have a main theme with subplots in the background, much like a made-for-TV disaster movie. Dreams are also very visual, so they use images to get their point across. The old saying "A picture is worth a thousand words" is very true with dreams. One image will tell you a lot more than "hearing" minutes worth of dialogue.

At one point in my own process of learning how to interpret dreams, I felt that I had just about nailed it. But my dreams themselves were telling me otherwise. I had a series of dreams where I was watching black-and-white movies in a movie theater. Eventually I realized that I was seeing my dreams in "black-and-white" and "two-dimensional." I was missing that the dreams were about many things, not just the main plot.

I am in a movie theater watching a black-and-white movie. I am off to the left side, looking at the screen from an angle. The movie is about popular rock bands, and it seems to be a documentary. Mom and Dad are behind me in the theater, although I don't actually see them. I just know that they are there. I wonder if they will enjoy this type of movie. It doesn't seem to be the kind of thing they would normally see.

With a typical interpretation, I would ask myself such questions as, "In what way are my parents behind me?" "How do I know they are behind me when I don't actually see them?" "What is the documentary of rock bands really about?" But there is much more to this dream, and that is where the black-and-white, two-dimensional movie watched from an angle comes in. Without understanding the meaning behind how I'm viewing this movie, I would only at best have a partial interpretation of this dream.

I have learned from experience with my own dreams to pay attention to the angles that I look at things from. I was on the left side of the theater, so I was only seeing the screen from one angle. In the weeks prior to this dream, I had several other dreams in which I was watching black-and-white movies. The term "black-and-white" to me means that I am seeing things only one way or another, with no in-between possibilities. I also realized that while watching a movie, we are seeing a flat screen (two dimensions). This was one of my first thoughts about this dream, and it led me to realize that I was missing much of what reality is.

Over the previous months I had gotten quite good at interpreting my dreams, and the results were fantastic. Still, there were always parts of dreams—symbolisms—that didn't make much sense, or that would show up a day or two later. My dreams were participating in my education, and I began to see that the imagery was a combination of past, present, and future symbols and events. When I reached this level of understanding, I had a dream that confirmed for me that I was on the right track.

I am standing outside on the lawn at night. I see a crescent moon and it has a tiny dark spot inside of it. I look again and the spot is now a bit larger and it has moved. Something now comes down from the sky. After a few moments I see that it is a woman on a surfboard, surfing down to Earth. She nearly hits my daughters as she gets close to the ground, but she goes a bit above and around them. After she lands, I now find myself sitting at a table with a dream-interpretation workbook. I have just completed Lesson One and am now ready to begin Lesson Two. Lesson Two starts out asking me to describe the two main focuses of this dream. There are blanks available for me to write my answers. I write down, "A woman surfs down to Earth" and "There is a dark spot inside of the moon."

After having this dream, I really felt as though my mind had validated for me what I had come to believe, and that is the multidimensional nature of dreams. It seems that dreams will help you with virtually anything that you want to learn, including helping you to interpret them.

REVIEW
Viewing your dreams in 3-D

1. **Learn the language.**
    Simply understanding that dreams have multiple meanings will help you to learn the language. Look at the dream as though it were a piece of art. What do you see? If you look at it from a different angle do you see something different?
2. **Write down your associations with symbols.**
    Pick an object, person, place, or event in the dream. Make a list of words and phrases that come to mind. For example: *movie theater, entertainment, fun, something I observe but don't interact with, popcorn, overpriced, celebrities, someplace I'd like to go more often.* After you make your list, see if any of those words or phrases match up with recent emotions. It is possible that the movie theater represents something or someone that I observe but do not interact with as well as something that I believe is overpriced. Those two things may or may not have anything to do with each other, yet both are valid interpretations.
3. **Notice how you observe things.**
    The word *see* is very general. How do you see? Is the image clear or blurry? Is it light or dark? Are you looking up, down, left, or right? Is something blocking your view? Do you like what you are seeing? Did the image change along the way? Does somebody else see something differently than you do? Are you seeing in color or black-and-white? Your answers will help you to understand how your dreams are constructed. If, for example, you are looking at something in black-and-white from an angle and the image turns into color upon changing your angle, your dream may be telling you that you have more options than what you have been seeing.

CHAPTER 4

Disproportionate objects

The mountain calls to me
With its snowcapped peaks higher than the clouds
And sheer cliffs beyond a human's ability to scale
It is high and mighty, yet beautiful and calm

But what gives rise most to my awe
Is that this morning that mountain was just a hill

If you pay attention, you will see that there are people, animals, houses, and other objects that are much larger in dreams than they are in real life. If you recognize a large symbol, you will get a big clue about the subject matter of the dream. Whatever it is that is exaggerated, it is attempting to call your attention to it.

> *I am standing in a shower that is located outside in an open field. I can see hills and trees around me. I realize that the shower is not pouring out water. It is pouring out something like a strawberry smoothie.*

This was a dream that my wife had that I was able to help her interpret. Initially she had no idea what this could have been about, but when I asked her to think of anything in the dream that may have been disproportionately large, she remembered that the showerhead was about the size of a sunflower. I asked her what her association with the word *shower* is, and she remembered a conversation that occurred at work the day before. We were planning our wedding at the time, and some of the people that she worked with discussed giving her a wedding shower and taking her out on the town. She was able at this point to identify the main theme of the dream. It was about a wedding shower and the conversation that occurred at her job. I asked her if there was anything in that conversation that made her uncomfortable in any way. She mentioned that her coworkers joked about taking her to strip clubs. Although she believed that it was just joking around, she also said that it wasn't really what she had in mind and realized that she did have a bit of discomfort about it. We ended up relating this to the strawberry smoothie. Sometimes when she and I go out, we order something like a smoothie rather than alcoholic drinks. The smoothie represented a more innocent choice. From there she was able to figure out the meaning of some smaller pieces of the dream and how it all related. Figuring out the theme was the key, and that was found by finding the oversized object.

The oversized symbol is not always an object. Sometimes it is an animal or a person. In the following example, I was able to figure out what three large dogs really represented.

> *I am outside at a park. I see my mother walking three very large dogs. Two of them are fluffy and look alike. The other looks like a bulldog. Mom is smiling and seems to be enjoying the walk. My dad is close to me. I walk up to him and ask him why Mom would want to take on that kind of responsibility. Dad said, "Because she fell in love with them the first time that she saw them."*

What stood out to me was the size of the dogs. The dogs didn't look familiar to me. My only association with dogs that I could think of is that I like them and have had a dog more often than not throughout my life. Still, the size of these dogs seemed to be calling my attention to them. So I considered what is in my life where there are two of something that are alike and one that is different but still similar. It didn't take me long to realize that the dogs represented my children——one boy and twin girls. Now that I understood that these dogs were really my children, the rest of the dream easily made sense. I am wondering why my mother would take on the responsibility and my father replies that it is because she loves them. Both of my parents are parts of my own personality. My mother represents the caregiver and my father represents logic. This dream was about the difficulty of parenting three children, pointing out that love is the reward. My mom and dad showed up as portions of my own personality because they are the best association I have with the word *parent*. As a side benefit, I then realized that my children could show up in my dreams as animals. I have seen my children show up as cats, a two-headed goat, and as various different kinds of dogs. Another way to think about oversized objects in a dream is to understand that it is the focal point of your dream. I believe this to be the easiest way to begin to interpret your dreams. If you find the exaggerated object, you will then find what the main theme of the dream is about.

Getting back to the shower dream, I had a related dream more than a year later. As you will see in many examples in this book, there were some strange similarities that occurred after the dream.

> *My wife and I are outside and our teenage daughter is waiting for us in our car. Our daughter then runs to us and says that a man came into the car while she was in there. I ran back and didn't find the man, but I found his wife. She says, "He doesn't hurt girls, he only looks at them." I say, "What difference does that make?" I yell at her about this and she eventually says, "I know," but I sense that she is in denial. I leave this place to go get some things at a store. I end up at a furniture store. My wife is there with a friend of hers. Next, I am driving and see a sign that I have entered the city of Minneapolis. I realize that I've gone too far and turn back to the suburb that I intended to go to. I get there and go into an apartment. My wife is there. There are two men who live in this place, although one of them isn't around. The other is walking around without his shirt on. He doesn't do anything blatantly to hit on my wife, but I feel that he's indirectly doing so. He makes it a point to bring her into his bathroom and show her his shower. The shower is just the showerhead with a small curtain that goes from the wall in a half circle.*

Two days after having this dream, my wife had lunch with her friend—the same one who was in this dream. My wife no longer worked at the job mentioned in the shower dream, but her friend still did. The friend mentioned to my wife that she found out that a man they used to work with was a sex offender, and his classification indicated the likelihood of his offenses being against a teen. This friend and the man they used to work with were the ones joking about taking my wife to strip clubs. It was the man, of course, who made me most uncomfortable. His wife was an employee at this same place, and in fact hired him. In the line of work they were in, he should not have been allowed to work at this place. After hearing about the discovery of this man being a sex offender, it matched up with a man going into our car with our daughter being in it. She is my first association with a teenager. My wife's friend showing up in the dream is odd in that she hadn't shown up in my dreams anytime recently that I could recall. I also was unaware that my wife was having lunch with her until the day after the dream. Next, we have the two men living together in an apartment. The building my wife used to work at with this man was, at one time, an apartment building. There was a second man who worked with them, although he was rarely there, much like in the dream. In the dream, the apartment was located in the same suburb that my wife's former job was at. The man walking around without his shirt off indicates my discomfort with the man, and feeling that he is subtly trying to hit on my wife. He didn't do anything blatantly to hit on my wife while they worked together, but I was never comfortable with him. My gut told me at the time that something wasn't right. Last, there was the shower. In the same conversation in which my wife found out that this man was a sex offender, she told her friend about her dream the year before with the shower and how I helped her to interpret the meaning.

The symbolisms and feelings of this dream totally matched up with my emotions after finding out that this man is a sex offender, even though the dream occurred before the event. The seemingly simple symbol of a showerhead turned out to have a lot of significant meaning, pointing out discomforts with a situation that ended up being validated.

REVIEW
Disproportionate objects

1. **Note any objects in your dream that are larger than they would be in real life.**
   If you have written down your dream, go back and highlight or underline the objects that you realize were larger than they should be. Often you may recall only one such object, in which case you probably have found the main theme of the dream. In the examples given in this chapter, I would highlight the word *shower* in one dream and *dogs* in the other.
2. **Does your vision in the dream focus on an object?**
   In addition to seeing something large, it is also common that your vision will focus in on this particular object in your dream. As you think back on your dream, pay attention to this. It is literally telling you what to focus on.
3. **What are your associations with this object?**
   Ultimately this is the important question. Paying attention to overly large objects can make it easy to find what you should focus on in order to interpret the dream, but in the end you will need to consider what that object means to you. I recommend that you write a list of your associations with this object. Don't think too hard. It is best to use free association and write anything that comes to mind. There is a good chance that you will see something that makes sense to you. In the shower example, you might write the words *clean, water, bathe, wedding, baby, gifts*. With a list like this, it would be easy for my wife to have remembered her conversation the day before about a wedding shower. Remember, the main focus of a dream often shows up as a disproportionately sized object. Of all of the methods of interpretation listed in this book, this is among the easier ones to learn and one of the best at finding out the true meaning of your dream.

CHAPTER 5

Lucid dreams

Flora of life
On boughs of divine
Essence of color
Resplendently shine

Vista of night
My lucid reverie
Thy brilliant light
'Tis I whilst 'tis thee

Lucid dreams are dreams in which you are aware that you are dreaming at the time that the dream is occurring. When you are aware that it is a dream, you can do anything that you want. You can fly, walk through walls, change the scenery, visit deceased people, have spiritual experiences, face your fears, heal yourself, prepare for some event, or just have fun. You may even be able to interpret your dream as it occurs. Lucid dreams can happen spontaneously, but generally they require some effort. I have found that if I make an effort to have more lucid dreams, the frequency of them increases. Some of my most wonderful and spiritual life experiences have occurred while having a lucid dream. There are some excellent books available to teach you techniques to induce lucid dreams. If you have never had a lucid dream, I would highly recommend that you make it a goal to have at least one. It may just change your life.

> *I am standing in a rather bare room. The floor is hardwood and there is a window across the room from where I am standing. Sunlight is coming in through the window. I realize that I am dreaming. The scene becomes crisper and the colors become more vivid. I walk across the room to the window and look out. I see a big open meadow. There is one tree on a small hill a distance out into the meadow. I look at it and now I can see it as though it is much closer. I see the entire tree, but*

*at the same time I am seeing individual leaves. The leaves are bright
green and they are glowing. I can see an aura of this bright green light
around each leaf. I realize that the entire tree is alive, but so too is each
individual leaf.*

I had this dream many years ago and I still remember it as though I had
it last night. It forever changed me. Through this dream, I saw a connection
between all living things. We are individuals, but we are all connected. This
dream left me with a sense of peace that lasted for a long time. I still have
peaceful feelings when I recall this dream. Ever since I had this dream, I look
at trees differently. I find myself often stopping to notice them. I listen to the
sound of the wind going through the leaves. I see the individual leaves in
the trees. I didn't do that before. Previously trees were just part of whatever
scenery that I was looking at. This dream didn't require analyzing it or trying
to interpret the images. I understood everything that I needed to immediately
upon awakening. That is a nice feeling.

Experiments can be fun to try in lucid dreams. As a teenager, I was curious
about how music would sound in a dream. I decided to try and listen to
music the next time that I had a lucid dream, and that opportunity came not
long after.

*I am outside of my house in the backyard. I remember that I haven't
lived at this house for a while. We moved a couple of years ago. I realize
that I must be dreaming. I remember that I intended to listen to music
the next time that I had a lucid dream. I make my stereo materialize
right in front of me. The stereo is sitting there on the lawn. I take a
cassette tape and I try to put it in the cassette deck. I can't get the tape
to fit. I try a couple of times unsuccessfully. Finally I just jam the tape
in there and then music begins to play by itself. I hear music like I've
never heard it before. The sound is coming from everywhere, as though
the air itself is producing it. It is very cool.*

I often have a tendency to want to fly when I first realize that I'm dreaming.
Think about what you might want to do when you realize that you are having
a dream. There is a good chance that you will remember your intention when
you do have a lucid dream.

REVIEW
Lucid dreams

1. **Read about them.**
    Learning to have lucid dreams is worthwhile. Until you experience one,
    it is hard to understand the feelings of freedom that you get from them.

I highly recommend reading a book or listening to an audio book about lucid dreams. Many people have their first lucid dream after reading or hearing about them.

2. **Record your lucid dreams.**

More than any other kind of dream, I suggest that you write down your lucid dreams. They have a tendency to be very positive and often spiritual experiences. My main reason for writing them down is not so much to interpret them but to preserve a wonderful memory.

3. **Experiment.**

Since nothing is impossible in a lucid dream, why not have fun with it? Think about something that you would like to do then next time that you have a lucid dream. If you indeed have a lucid dream, you may very well remember your intention. Consider asking yourself a question about something that you really want to know. You may learn a lot about yourself.

CHAPTER 6

Actions and figures of speech

Dreams
Represent
Explanations
Acronyms
Metaphors
Symbols

The verbs used to describe your dreams are very important in deciphering the meaning. After I journal my dreams, I often go back and highlight action words. When looking at the action, forget about the symbols for the moment. Forget about the people, places, and other things going on. Just ask yourself in the most basic terms, "What was I doing?"

> *I am standing on a golf course with no grass. It is muddy. The sky is cloudy. I have a putter in my hand. I am taking a long shot. I hit the ball and it stretches out like slime and oozes into the hole. Now the course is green and beautiful and the sky is sunny.*

When highlighting action phrases, eliminate the nouns and just look at the action. Sometimes I replace the noun with a pronoun to help focus on the action. "I am standing," "I have something in my hand," "I am taking a long shot," "I hit something," "Something oozes."

Dreams often use figures of speech, metaphors, and other plays on words in the form of imagery. Looking at my highlighted list of actions, the one that stuck out to me was "I am taking a long shot." This dream was not about golf. Heck, I have never golfed in my life. It was about taking a long shot. What would I want to be taking a long shot at? I thought about what the ball did when I hit it. It oozed like slime. As it turns out, at that time in my life I had been considering starting a small candy- and gumball-machine business. The ball oozed like slime, or perhaps like a chewed up gumball. I made the shot and everything became all beautiful and sunny. This dream was telling me to take a long shot on the business and it would turn out well. I listened to this dream and had fun with that little sideline business. During that same week, I had another dream in which I had taken a long shot in a basketball game and made the shot. My dreams during that week were trying to find different ways to tell me to take a shot.

You may not always be the person in the dream doing the action, but in reality it is still you.

> *I am at a restaurant and the president of the United States walks in. He comes to our table and shakes hands with me and others at the table. I have a camera with me and I hand it to a guy across the table so that he can take my picture with the president. He tried to take the picture but he wasn't getting the camera to work.*

It took me a lot of thought to figure out the guy with the camera. I kept thinking that the camera was broken, so I was asking myself, "What is broken?" I wasn't making the connection. So I thought really hard about the dream to try and figure out what part of the camera was broken. I realized that the camera wasn't broken at all. The guy couldn't figure out how to make it work. So, I thought of the phrase *He couldn't figure out how to make it work.* Then it made sense. I had been trying to think of ways financially for my wife (then my girlfriend) to move long-distance to be with me. I couldn't figure out how to make it work. From there I was able to interpret other symbolisms, which essentially told me that we wouldn't have a lot of financial security, but we would have enough. Within a few months we were engaged and living together in a nicer home than I would have expected.

Every so often I have been able to figure out an acronym. These can be tricky, but very interesting if you are able to find them in a dream. It certainly goes to show just how creative dreams can be.

> *I am in a crowded restaurant and suddenly realize that I'm dreaming. I remember thinking about my financial problems before going to sleep, feeling at a total loss for how to handle it. I go up to the first person that I see, who is a teenage boy, and I ask him for help. I am having trouble speaking much louder than a whisper. I realize that my stress about this issue is preventing me from communicating about it very effectively. After this realization I ask again and I'm able to speak somewhat louder, but I now I can't hear him very well. I decide to use yes-or-no questions and I ask him if my stress about my finances is the*

problem. He nods yes, but he has a look in his eye as though there is more, so I ask him if there is more to it. He nods yes again. I decide to find someone else to talk to. I turn around and there is a very large man who looks like a biker. He is quite intimidating looking, but I am aware that this is a dream and I feel that it is a good opportunity to confront fear and talk to him anyway. I say to him, "I don't know how to handle my financial problems. I need help." He responds saying, "Ask the old man." I then walk through the front window of the restaurant and fly before the dream ends.

I found many parts of this dream that gave me some answers to the question that I was asking, but ultimately it was what the biker told me that caused me to really get it. Of course I had partially received my answer from the teenage boy. It was true that my stress was making it difficult for me to come up with a positive answer, and it is hard to communicate effectively while you are stressed. But that still left a lot of questions. Initially my thoughts were of my dad. I wondered if the dream was suggesting that I either ask my dad for advice, or literally ask him for some money. But why would he be referred to as the old man? I never call him "Old Man." I know enough about dreams to understand that this is not accidental. If I were meant to ask my dad for advice or money, the dream would have used a character and wording more in line with that idea. I considered the possibility of an acronym with the words "ask the Old Man," or "ATOM." I thought about atoms and realized that the night before I had been reading a chapter in a book by Dr. Wayne Dyer in which he mentioned molecules. Dr. Dyer is among my favorite authors and, on occasion, he has shown up in my dreams as a sort of higher version of me. At this point I understood that the old man was not my father, but Dr. Dyer—who happens to be approximately the same age as my father (which is something that I had mentally noted on more than one occasion). My dream was intentionally using the term *Old Man* so as to differentiate Dr. Dyer from my father. I have gained so much from Dr. Dyer's books and audios that in some ways he does feel like a father figure to me, even though we've never met. So, what my dream character was telling me when he said "Ask the old man" is that I should take advice from Dr. Dyer—at least figuratively speaking. I asked myself, "What would Wayne Dyer do in this situation?" Instantly I heard an answer inside of my mind. It said, "Say to the universe that I don't know the correct path to take in this situation" and then trust that the universe will provide me with what I need. Most importantly, I had that feeling of nailing the dream interpretation. I knew that I got this right and indeed I felt much better. A valuable lesson came from this dream. The dream did not tell me literally how to go out and make more money, but rather it chose to focus on getting my emotions in healthier shape and to have faith in something greater than myself. Even as I am writing this book, I am still having a lot of financial problems. Admittedly I still do get stressed about it. But somewhere in the back of my mind, I have this "blind" faith that everything is as it is supposed to be. I believe that this struggle is in my life at this moment because it is redirecting me to places that I would never go had it not been a part of my life.

Something further strange occurred in relation to this last dream example. A couple of nights prior to writing this I had a dream in which I was driving with an old man sitting in the passenger seat. This man had an aura of wisdom about him, but he didn't ever say anything. He let me figure things out for myself related to problems that I was having driving. I had been able to figure out much of the other symbolisms in this dream, but I hadn't placed the meaning behind the old man until the following night. I hadn't intended to do any writing that night, but I had gotten my daughters to bed and my wife was in our room reading a book to my son. I also had been having some trouble sleeping the previous few nights and figured it might be good to stay up a bit later to make sure that I was sufficiently tired before turning in. So I decided to read through some notes that I had for this book. One of those notes to myself was to include something about acronyms. I immediately knew which dream example that I wanted to use, so as it turns out I ended up writing the "Old Man" example in this chapter. As I got to the part in the dream where the large man says, "Ask the old man," my previous night's dream entered my mind and I suddenly understood who the old man is. He is that same higher, wiser part of me that Dr. Dyer also represented. I found this very strange, because I had no intention of doing any writing this night, yet it was the writing that caused me to make the connection. It felt as if something in my mind had orchestrated this whole thing, from the dream in the car with the old man to writing about Dr. Dyer (the old man). Is it possible that my subconscious set me up to have insomnia so that I'd be up later than normal, and then have the acronyms part of my notes stand out over the rest? Of course I had no way of knowing that my wife and son would also be up late reading and thereby occupying my bed. And to make this even more interesting, the following night I had been reading *The Zahir* by Paulo Coelho, and in the final page of the chapter I was in were the words, "History will only change when we are able to use the energy of love, just as we use the energy of the wind, the seas, the atom." Seeing the word *atom,* along with the context in which it was used, matched so well with everything else that I was left with this feeling that all of it indeed was orchestrated just for me. The only question is, by whom?

Now, this story isn't yet over. Two days later I drove for the first time following surgery two weeks earlier. The first place that I went was to my daughter's school. She called in the morning needing something from home. My wife would have been late for work, so I decided to go seeing as I'd been given the okay to drive. My daughter and I got home at about the same time that day and she asked me to take her to the library to get a book that she needed to research a school paper. She was only aware that I was able to drive because I'd gone to her school that morning. Otherwise she would have waited until her mother came home and asked her. And had she asked me even one day earlier I would not have been able to take her. But as things turned out, I was both available to take her and given permission by my doctor to do so.

There was nothing that I wanted at the library, having just recently checked out two other books. Since I was there, however, I figured that I might as well look around while I was waiting for my daughter. Near the back of the library I saw a display of new nonfiction books. There was a book about promoting personal wealth that caught my eye, but I had not had a chance to look at it when my daughter said that she was ready to go. I decided to just check out the book and see what it was about when I got home. We walked down an aisle of audiobooks on the way to the checkout desk, and there was one large-sized audiotape box that was sticking out much further than all the others on that shelf. The audio book was *There's a Spiritual Solution to Every Problem* by Dr. Wayne Dyer. That is the book that provided me with the answer that I found in my "Ask the old man" dream. I began reading the finance book when I got home, and the ideas I found in this book were familiar to me, made a lot of sense, and gave me the feeling that I did have some control over my situation. This all started with a thought about wanting to find a solution to my financial problems. From there I had a lucid dream that reminded me to think about what Dr. Wayne Dyer would do, which I determined was to let the universe do what it does and trust that the answer would appear. A few months later I have another dream that reminds me of the first, and I end up writing about it because my bedroom is occupied and I have insomnia. Then I read in another book about unconditional love and atoms, which is strikingly similar to the message in my dream and from where that message came. And, by chance, I end up unexpectedly at the library a couple of days later and check out a personal-finance book that I had no idea even existed, then walk past the very same Wayne Dyer audio that gave me my initial answer (inside of a dream) in the first place.

At the risk of sounding like an infomercial, but wait, there's more! Among my various financial woes was a problem with my house that was going to cost a fair amount of money to repair. I talked with my father about this and on his own he made a phone call to a handyman whom he had gotten to know and trust from recent work on his own home. The handyman came out to my house and called the next day with an offer to make the repair at one-third the cost of estimates I had received elsewhere. On top of that, my parents offered to pay that cost. As it turns out, I really did end up asking my father (along with the old man) for help and he was able to find a deal that I never could have on my own. This household repair deal, by the way, happened to occur on the exact same day that I went to the library and found the financial book. My dad hadn't yet met the handyman at the time of my initial dream, so he would not have been able to provide the same help at that time. The timing for everything was truly incredible. In the end, the solutions to my problem were literally manifested in the form of a book, and in the form of a handyman unknown at the time of the initial dream.

REVIEW
Actions and figures of speech

1. **Write the first thing that comes to your mind.**

   When writing down your dreams, don't edit them. Just let your hand move on the paper or let your fingers click on the keyboard. Don't second-guess yourself. It may be that initial choice of words that interprets your dream. If you change your wording to something that "sounds better," you may in the process hurt your chances for interpretation.

2. **Highlight action phrases.**

   The action phrases are telling you what you, or others, are doing. Even if it sounds really bizarre, don't worry about it. What you are looking for is what, at the most basic level, you are doing. The long-shot dream makes a good example of this. Don't worry about the club that I was holding, what the scenery looked like, or what I was hitting. By eliminating the details, I narrowed it down to "I am taking a long shot." Dreams very often will use figures of speech or slang to make a point.

3. **Ask yourself how this phrase relates to a current situation in your life.**

   If you understand what you were doing in the dream at the most basic level, think about how this relates to any current situation in your life. The phrase you highlight may be a metaphor, a phrase, or even just a single word. The idea is to make a comparison with just that word or phrase with your actual life. In my camera dream, after giving it some thought I realized that the man couldn't figure out how to make it work. So the question that I asked myself was, "In what way am I having trouble figuring out how to get something to work?" Remember, dreams tend to be very current, so think about what was on your mind the previous day.

CHAPTER 7

Communication devices

Be silent and the universe will speak to you

L earning what symbols mean to you will make it easier to interpret dreams as you go on. It is like learning a foreign language in that it does get easier over time. Symbols can change their meaning to you over time, but even so the general concept behind those symbols tend to remain much the same.

Although each person needs to determine for him or herself what personal dream symbols mean, there are many symbols that have a fairly universal meaning in our society. One of them is telephones and other communication devices. This may include cellular phones, radios, and televisions.

These symbols all have communication in common. Some are two-way communication and others are one-way. Sometimes you have good reception and other times you don't. Some are portable and others are stationary. Sometimes you dial out, other times someone calls you. Some are visual and others only verbal.

Knowing that these devices represent communication to me, I have an early clue to help me decipher the dream. They often represent communication issues that I'm having with someone. Someone may not be hearing what I'm trying to say, or perhaps I'm not receiving his or her message. Maybe someone is talking too loud. If you play around with the verbs, you often can make sense of these communication dreams.

My wife and I are guests in someone's home. We are sitting in their living room. There are two couches next to each other making an L-shape. I am sitting on one couch and my wife is on the other. There is a TV in front of each of us. The news is on. We are both watching the same thing, but I am watching the TV in front of me and she is

*watching the TV in front of her. The TV that I am watching is getting
a bit better reception and is a bit larger than the one that s
he is watching.*

My wife and I had an argument the day before. We both had been under
a fair amount of stress and we let out some things on each other. Looking at
this dream, we were sitting in the same room but facing different directions.
We each were watching the same thing on TV. That means we were
essentially looking at the same thing, but seeing it from different angles. So
when we had our argument, each of us was only looking at it from our own
angle. In this case my TV had slightly better reception and the screen was
bigger. In real life, I had been able to see even during this stressful argument
that it was just a bad day. Upset as I was, I knew this wasn't the end of the
world and that we all have "one of those days." In the dream, I was able to see
the "bigger picture" and the lack of distortion on the TV was also confirming
this. Yet at the same time, the dream also was telling me that there are two
sides to everything. We both can be seeing and hearing the same thing, but
interpret it differently. There doesn't have to be a right or wrong.

REVIEW
Communication devices

1. **List any communication devices that you see in your dream.**
   Communication issues are one of the biggest reasons for emotional
   difficulties that we all face. By noticing communication devices in your
   dreams, you will have a clue when you have some work to do in that area
   of your life. Consider how you would describe the following items to
   someone who is totally unfamiliar with what they are: telephone, cellular
   phone, television, radio, stereo, speakers, two-way radio, satellite. You may
   find several others on your own.

2. **Pay attention to which direction the communication is going.**
   The type of device that shows up in your dream tells you much about
   where your communication problems are coming from. Is someone
   calling you, or are you calling him or her? Is the device meant to be two-
   way communication, or does it only receive or send? In the example from
   this chapter, a television is a device that only receives. This dream was
   explaining to me how my wife and I were receiving information from the
   other.

3. **How good is the reception?**
   In communication dreams, it is common that you may have poor reception
   on whatever device you are using. If you are having trouble hearing
   someone, consider in what ways you might not be doing a good job of
   listening. If someone is having a hard time hearing you, then perhaps you

need to change your approach with that person. If the object is broken, then perhaps it is not going to be possible to have effective communication with someone, or there is serious work to be done.

CHAPTER 8

Fingerprints
of the mind

Sifted through the filters of our perceptions
We breathe the same air

There are tons of dream dictionaries out there. I'm not a fan of them, because dream symbols are very personal. Each person's mental association to certain objects is as individual as a fingerprint, so ultimately you will need to determine your own meaning. I will say that some dream dictionaries can be helpful to the extent they get you to think about an object in a way that you hadn't considered, and on occasion that can put you on the right track. Some symbols are more universal than others. People who live in the same society will have similar associations to certain items. The communication equipment is a good example. My association with a cell phone or television is probably not too dissimilar from yours. That is why many of us have similar symbolisms in our dreams. Cars are common in dreams, but obviously that wouldn't have been the case centuries ago. Today, they are an everyday part of our lives. Even with these common symbols, people's associations will have some degree of variation. My experiences with a cell phone may be positive, yours negative. You may use a cell phone for business, I use one for personal reasons. I may use a cell phone frequently to chat, while you keep it around only for emergencies. You had an easy time figuring out how to use your phone and I got frustrated trying to understand the darn thing. You prefer to use a hands-free attachment. I keep mine attached to my hip with a belt clip. So even so-called universal symbols may only have similar meaning to us on a surface level.

Once you have interpreted the meaning of a symbol in one dream, there is a high likelihood that the symbol will have a similar meaning in future dreams, thereby making interpretations easier as time goes on. The meaning of a symbol probably won't be exactly the same, and over time your associations with that symbol may evolve. However, from what I have experienced the basic meaning remains much intact over time.

> *I am negotiating the sale of my candy machines to a woman who responded to an ad that I had running in the paper. She doesn't have money to buy them, so she offers to make a trade. I ask her what she has and she says that she has many things. She mentions a couple of them and I am not interested. I suggest that if she fences my yard, I will trade the candy machines for that. We are outside looking at the yard. Two sides are already fenced in, but the rest of it needs to be done so that the yard is enclosed. I now notice that the unfenced side does have a fence, but it is not in my yard. This fence is well into the neighbor's yard. This doesn't work well, so I tell her that I want to put up a fence right on the property line where it should be.*

My wife had been helping out a friend who had some personal problems. I had been feeling that my wife was helping this friend too much.

Dreams aren't going to tell you what other people should be doing, or how they ought to be feeling. That is not in your control. Your dreams will assist you with how to best handle a situation within the scope of what you can do to help yourself. With that in mind, this dream is not about either my wife or her friend, but rather it is about my feelings and what I can do to create a less stressful situation for me.

When I looked at the symbol of what a fence is, my first association is that it is a boundary. It is a dividing line between one place and another. In the dream, I want someone to help me construct a boundary. A boundary is already there, but it is too far away from where I want it to be. I want the boundary moved right on the property line, "where it should be." While interpreting this dream, I asked myself these questions: What is it that I'm feeling? What is it that I want? How am I going to accomplish that?

The answer to the first questions is that I am feeling that a boundary of our personal lives is set someplace that is making me uncomfortable. So what do I really want? What I want in the dream is to put the fence right on the property line where I feel that it should be. This is a more loaded symbol than it first seems. It is one thing to determine where the fence currently is, but I also have to look at where it is that I want it to be. It is good that I want it right on the property line where it should be. That says that I am not trying to put it too far over one way or the other. If I had wanted the new fence constructed further into our yard, that could be saying that I am attempting to be too controlling by keeping my family closer. Right on the property line indicates that I truly want what is right, even if I don't know what that is. So how am I going to accomplish that? This dream tells me that I am trading the fence for something else of value to me. In fact, I titled this dream "Trade Off." I am telling myself that compromise will be needed. There is something that is important to me, and something else that I'm willing to trade off for it. The main message behind this dream is that there is a way for me to get what I want in a way that is fair to everyone.

Having interpreted a previous dream about fences some months earlier, this later dream was easy for me to figure out. However, there was more to it than it seemed at the time of the dream. A couple of days prior to this dream, this same friend of my wife's was at our house. She and I were talking and I mentioned to her that I would like to fence the yard, but it was too expensive to do right now. She mentioned to me that she had put up an inexpensive fence by digging and concreting the posts herself, then stretching something like a chicken-wire fence. So the symbolism of fences in my dream was a combination of my associations with fences being boundaries as well as from this recent conversation. Interestingly, the same day that I had this dream, I had gone out for a long jog and I went by a house where someone was constructing a new fence on just one side of their yard. The other sides were completed and there was an existing fence on the third side. However, the existing fence was well into their yard and they had put up posts to extend the fence right by the property line. And, believe it or not, the space between where the old fence was and where the new one was being constructed was filled in with chicken wire fencing.

REVIEW
Fingerprints of the mind

1. **Pay attention to symbols that repeat themselves in your dreams.**
   If a symbol shows up repeatedly in your dreams, it clearly is trying to tell you something. If you can figure out what that symbol means to you, then you will have a much better chance of interpreting your dreams. You should see that you have symbolisms that show up over and over again. These symbols are often objects, but they could also be people, places, sounds, or even thoughts.
2. **Create your own dream dictionary.**
   Note down the name of the symbol and what that symbol means to you. Write down whatever associations you have with that object. It may be easiest to start by looking at physical objects, such as a fence in my example. Using a fence as a symbol for my own personal dream dictionary, I would make my entry something like this:

FENCE:
- Used to create a boundary
- Used for privacy

- Separates one thing from another

Now that I have noted down my association with fences, I have something to begin an interpretation within each subsequent dream in which a fence appears. Anytime that I see a fence in a dream, I can make a safe assumption that there is some boundary issue. Once you figure out the meaning of an object, the more likely it is to appear in future dreams. Your mind wants you to have the ability to interpret your dreams.

CHAPTER 9

Who are
your parents?

Complicating what I see
Is that my mom and dad are me
But how is it that this can be?
Should the number not add up to three?

Learning who people are in your dreams can be more confusing than figuring out objects. People sometimes are themselves, but they often represent aspects of your own personality. You can gain clues about their meaning in the dream based on the situations in which you see these people. For example, someone from work may represent your business life. You might associate someone as being funny, in which case they represent your sense of humor.

Parents are among the most complex people symbols that you will dream about. They are people that you have known for your entire life, and your relationship with them has changed quite a lot over the years. No doubt you have a lot of strong feelings about them, one way or the other.

I have noticed that my parents have shown up more in my dreams since I had children of my own. They are my symbol for the word *parents*. Sometimes it is only one of my parents, and sometimes both of them are part of the dream. Sometimes they converse with each other or with me, and other times I am simply an observer watching what they are doing.

I am driving with Mom and Dad in the backseat. I don't see them but I know that they are there. I feel like this has been a long trip. I take a corner too quickly and go over a curb. I slow down and make some comment about having gone too fast, but Mom and Dad don't seem to notice. I am now out of the car looking at it. It is an old Gremlin with a little spare tire on the front driver's side.

At this time of my life, I was going through my divorce. My life felt very out of control in many ways, and yet I had to keep doing my job as a parent even when I was tired and didn't feel up to it. My parents are me in this dream. They are the parenting part of my personality. The "me" in this dream is the person who is having trouble keeping things under control. My parents are able to remain calm even though the car is going too fast. I was doing fine parenting despite the chaos.

Besides the main plot, I was able to make out some of the behind-the-scenes multiple meanings in this dream. The Gremlin with the bad front driver's side tire was a warning to me. A few days after this dream, I was out of town and about ready to head back home when I noticed my car making a strange sound. I ended up borrowing a family member's car to get home and had mine brought into a shop. As it turns out, a bolt had fallen out of the brake in the front driver's side of the car, causing the caliper to hang free. It would have been quite dangerous to drive on it, particular on a long-distance drive.

REVIEW
Who are your parents?

1. **Consider that your parents may be aspects of yourself.**
    If you are a parent, your own parents will be your closest association with the word *parent*. More specifically, the words *mother* and *father* may represent that aspect of your life. In the case of my parents, my mother tends to be emotional and my father logical. Which parent shows up in my dream has much to do with that aspect of their personalities.

2. **What are your parents doing in the dream?**
    The actions of your parents in the dream will give you additional clues about their symbolism. In my example, my parents were in the backseat of the car. This represents them not being in control. I could ask myself (and I did), how do I feel out of control with my parenting right now? Maybe you are fighting with your parents in the dream, or perhaps your parents are doing nothing to help you. In a more positive dream, your parents may be the ones to help you out of a difficult situation.

3. **What is your real-life relationship with your parents?**
    This part is the biggest clue to determine who your parents are in your dream. Obviously a person who was raised in an abusive home is going to have a significantly different experience of what a parent is than someone who was raised in a loving and safe home. So, think about how you feel around your parents. Do you feel like you can always count on them, like a safety net? Do they make you feel like none of your ideas are good? Do you feel compared to your siblings? Do you feel like you don't live up to

their expectations? Are your parents married, divorced, or were you raised by a single parent? Do you still feel like a child when you are around them? Asking these types of questions will help you to make sense of your parents as symbols in your dreams.

CHAPTER 10

The supporting cast

If you understand these lines that be
Then you know the real me
But the real me is he, you see
Or her or him or we or thee

The real me can sometimes fly
And perhaps you'll see him in the sky
If falls to earth he will not die
But sometimes he won't even try

No wealth or fame or success by trade
But rich at times without being paid
Poor at times when it all seems to fade
In either case no doubt self-made

Do you question what you see?
He might have climbed up David's tree
But could have gone to Italy
The man that is the real me

Trying to determine who dream characters really are can be confusing. Sometimes they are the people that they seem to be. It is possible that your spouse in a dream really represents your spouse. On the other hand, that person may represent some part of your own personality, such as the friend of yours that has a lot of money representing your symbolism for how you feel about your finances.

Over time I have come to see that the larger the role that a person plays in your dreams, the more likely they are to represent an aspect of your own personality. Those people that are "extras" in the dream, like the background people in a movie, may really represent part of the scene and not so much an actual person.

> *I am in a restaurant. I order the special, which is stuffed shoe. The shoe is a brown leather dress shoe stuffed with fluffy cotton-looking material. I go to pay the girl at the cash register. She is young and seems friendly.*

The night before I had this dream, I had gone to the grocery store and picked up just a few things. The young lady in the checkout line handled a difficult customer ahead of me very well, and then was friendly with a smile when I got to the counter. I was impressed with how she handled herself. It started raining hard as I was in the checkout line, and I didn't have an umbrella with me. After bagging my groceries, I walked out of the store and slowly walked to my car, getting soaked by the rain. I really enjoyed it. I felt no need to run or to wait it out. I felt an odd sense of peace while walking slowly through the rain.

In my dream, the lady at the cash register really did represent the lady at the grocery store cash register. It is nobody that I personally know, so essentially she was part of the scenery. It helped me make a connection to the grocery store experience.

The shoe part was related to a book on tape that I was listening to earlier in the day about dreams. The author had mentioned symbolism, using shoes as an example. Shoes can be many things, one of which is that they have soles (souls). That statement stuck with me for a minute after hearing it. You could say that I found peace, or made a connection to my soul, by walking into a rainstorm and allowing myself to enjoy getting soaked.

REVIEW
The supporting cast

1. **How big a role does a specific person play in your dream?**
    If a person in your dream has a major role, consider the possibility that this person represents some aspect of yourself. If you are looking into the meaning of a character with a small role, write down anything that strikes you about this person in your dream. Note what they look like and what their personality is like, what they are doing, and your interaction with them, if any. Then give some thought to your previous day and see if you can recall someone similar. It could be the clerk at the post office, a client that you met at a business meeting, someone who held the door open for you, etc.
2. **What is your association with the person in question?**
    A person with a larger role may be someone that you have extensive history with, such as a family member, a friend, or your boss. It can be

dream, but my dream still answered.

I had learned from previous experience, such as my big-dogs dream, that the pattern of two plus one represents my children. I have a son and twin daughters. That pattern has shown up frequently in my dreams. Therefore I was able to recognize that the money represented my children. Initially I saw two one-dollar bills and then noticed a third one. There is my two-plus-one pattern. Behind that I saw a five-dollar bill. In this dream I was hoping to give away three dollars and keep the five. With my girlfriend and her daughter, I would have five with me instead of three. So, there is the meaning behind the five-dollar bill. I am hoping the students will answer correctly. I want to be able to give them three and keep five.

I had to consider that I had fake money in one of my hands, and think about the possibility that the fake money represented something fake. In order to determine the real meaning, I asked myself which hand the real money was in. It was in the right hand. There was my answer.

REVIEW
Number patterns

1. **Write down the numbers that show up in your dreams.**
   The best way to start understanding the meaning of numbers in your dreams is to pay attention to them and to write them down. It may take more than one dream to understand the meaning. As you begin to see patterns, you will start learning what certain numbers or combinations of numbers mean to you. Make sure that you don't just write down the number, but also how it shows up. In my money example, I would note that I saw two, then one, and then five. If I instead wrote down that I had eight dollars, I would never have figured out the accurate meaning.

2. **What do these numbers mean to you?**
   With each number that you see, write down as many associations as you can. See how many of those numbers match up with areas of your life. This could include the number of people in your family, the number of people that you work with, how many items you have in a collection, etc. A big clue here is that an individual number may be hard for you to determine its symbolism, but an equation or series of numbers together may make sense. The numbers one or two alone would mean little to me as there are far too many possibilities with those individual numbers. However, the one-plus-two combination was something much easier to see.

CHAPTER 12

Your dream wardrobe

Underdressed for a formal affair
They do not notice or seem to care

Why then do you?

Clothing or lack thereof in dreams represents figuratively what you are wearing. What other people are wearing is also something to pay close attention to. Dreams of being naked, underdressed, or inappropriately dressed often point out feelings of exposure or self-consciousness. It isn't actually the clothing making you feel this way, but it is a way for the dream to point it out. How would you feel if you were only partially dressed in public? You might be embarrassed, or you might wish you were elsewhere. It is those feelings that matter. The choice of clothing always has a meaning. Sometimes the clothing is the main focus, and much of the time it is part of the scenery that you don't pay as much attention to. In the following example, the clothing is the focus of the dream and what I used to interpret it.

> *I am at someone's house on the lower level. There are many people*
> *there for an event. It turns out to be a wedding. I see the bride. She is*
> *wearing her wedding dress, but the front of it is open so that her bare*
> *chest is fully exposed. My brother is going to be marrying her, and he*
> *doesn't seem to take notice of the odd dress.*

To me, a wedding dress is a fairly strong symbol for the word *marriage.* What I took this dream to mean is that something was being exposed in the marriage. The groom, in this case played by my brother, wasn't noticing this exposure. This dream occurred while I was still married to my ex-wife. My brother represented a part of me that wasn't seeing something in the marriage that should have been blaringly obvious. The "me" in the dream was able to see it. Not long after this, I slowly started to question a lot of things in my marriage that didn't seem right to me. Many things were in fact exposed. My mind was preparing me to start seeing some things that consciously I didn't want to look at, but that I needed to know.

In the next example, I am without clothing during a portion of the dream.

> *I am at a house with my wife and daughter. A business similar to the one my wife works at is operating in this house. The house is being remodeled and therefore the business is closed at the moment. My wife decides to apply for a job there anyway, since the owners are there. They bring her in for an interview. During this time, my daughter and I explore the house. I end up by myself, and I assume my daughter to be exploring a different part of the house. I am upstairs in a hallway near a bedroom and a bathroom. There is a man in the bedroom. I realize that I am now naked. I am not self-conscious of it, but I would prefer to have clothes on because I think it is making the man uncomfortable. Somehow I know that my daughter is naked too, even though I don't know where she is.*

During the time of this dream, my wife was dealing with some significant job stress. She would often come home feeling stressed or drained. I was having a difficult time not allowing those feelings to rub off on me. Sometimes I would find myself trying to do too much around the house to ease her stress, and other times I just felt bad because we would go longer periods of time without as much laughter and smiles.

In the dream, the house is a similar business to the one my wife works at, indicating the connection to her job. She is interviewing while our daughter and I are exploring the house. This represents my wife dealing with her job, while our daughter and I are each "exploring" on our own what this is all about. I had been feeling that our oldest daughter, the one in this dream, had also been affected by the job stress. That is where the nakedness comes in. Where our daughter is concerned, she was off exploring on her own, and I felt that she was as "exposed" to this as I was. As for me, I was more concerned with the discomfort of another person than I was with my own nakedness. I understood what this meant. I felt that my own feelings about this issue were upsetting my wife even further. It didn't bother me to talk about it, but I felt that my efforts to do so weren't helping. Symbolically speaking, I felt like it would be best to put some clothes back on and not let the other person see me naked. That means that I felt like it would be best not to expose my own emotions so much, because they were making her uncomfortable. That discomfort, in turn, made me more uncomfortable as well. The lesson in this dream is that part of communication is to know when not to say some things.

REVIEW
Your dream wardrobe

1. **Be specific about the clothing that you are describing.**
    In order to determine what the clothing represents, it isn't enough to say "blue shirt" or "jeans." There usually will be something about the clothing that stands out to you if you think about it. The article of clothing is unusually bulky, or it exposes more than you are comfortable with. You might be missing part of your outfit, or there is a hole in it. Perhaps it is something that you would never wear in real life, or you are seeing someone dressed inappropriately for the situation.
2. **Describe the purpose of this particular article of clothing.**
    Some clothing is meant for comfort, some for business, and some for recreational activity. Coats keep you warm, and shorts keep you cool. The wedding dress, as in my example, represents marriage. A cloak or trench coat might be used to cover up something.
3. **Note other people's reactions to your clothing.**
    Naked or partially clothed dreams are very common. If you have such a dream, pay attention to the reactions of your other dream characters. For me, most of the times the other people in my dream don't even seem to notice. This indicates that I am self-conscious of something that is not obvious to anyone else. If everyone does notice, then whatever issue you are dealing with is probably obvious to other people.

CHAPTER 13

Short dreams have meaning

Since we can only live the present moment
Is not an instant and eternity the same thing?

One misconception about dream interpretation is that you need to remember a lengthy and detailed dream in order to be able to decipher any meaning from it. That is simply not true. In fact, it is often easier interpret the meaning behind dream symbols when you are not so confused by large numbers of images. A couple of seconds of a dream can be interpreted. You may even me able to derive some meaning behind a single image.

I see two dolphins swimming in a dolphin pool at the zoo. The dolphins are wearing glass bubbles over their heads.

My entire memory of this dream is a matter of a few seconds, yet it was enough to understand the meaning. One of the things that I considered about this dream was that I was at a zoo. The day before, I had been driving with my twin daughters and I had children's music playing for them. One of the songs was called "At the Zoo." Normally I would have had my son with me at that time of day, but on this day I happened only to have the twins with me. Having recognized where the zoo scenery came from, and knowing that my children often show up in my dreams as animals, I understood that the dolphins were my daughters.

Okay, so now I understood where the zoo symbolism came from and who the dolphins were, but what was this dream trying to tell me? I thought about the clear glass bubbles on the dolphins' heads. They seemed to be some kind of breathing apparatus or protective gear, not unlike what an astronaut might use. I know that dolphins are mammals and can breathe out of the water. They don't need this protective gear. I took that to mean that there is some way in which my daughters don't need protection from something. As I thought about the previous couple of days, one of the things that had been in the back of my mind was that my daughters were moving into a new day-care room. There were two possible teachers that they might have ended up with, and it was possible that they could be split into different rooms for the first time. I was familiar with one of the teachers, whom I liked. I was not too familiar with the other teacher. As it turns out, they did both end up in the same classroom, but with the teacher that I didn't know as well. I ended up feeling good about the choice that the day care made. Both girls did very well with this teacher. These few seconds of dream memory were enough to tell me that my daughters were going to be fine. They didn't need me to overprotect them.

REVIEW
Short dreams have meaning

1. **Describe the image.**
   It may be only a single image, but you might be surprised at just how much detail you can gain from it. A picture truly is worth a thousand words. Even if my image of the dolphins had been a still image, like a photograph, I would have been able to describe the pool, the dolphins, and the bubbles on their heads.

2. **What stands out as odd in this image?**
   In my example, the bubbles on the dolphins' heads were out of place. The dolphin pool and the dolphins themselves looked normal. But in real life you would not see dolphins wearing glass bubbles on their heads. So that is what the dream was calling my attention to. Once you have determined the odd image, describe it. I described the glass bubbles as something similar to what an astronaut would use to breathe. I realized immediately that this is unnecessary for a dolphin.

3. **Use other standard interpretation techniques.**
   The length of a dream has nothing to do with the effectiveness of an interpretation technique. I am aware from experience that my children often show up in my dreams as animals, and I know to look for certain numbers or number patterns in my dreams. It was easy for me to make the connection that the twin dolphins in the dream were in fact my twin daughters. Even if this dream had been much longer, I still would have used the same techniques to determine who the dolphins were and what they were trying to tell me.

CHAPTER 14

Intense dreams

I live, I hope, I dream, I pray
I watch, I learn, I work, I play

I feel, I know, I sense, I cry
I sleep, I wake, I laugh, I die

From my own experiences, I have seen a difference between early night and morning dreams. For one thing, we are much more likely to remember a morning dream. The dream is much more recent, plus we are in a lighter state of sleep. If you keep a journal by the bed and make it a point to jot down your dream memories during the night, you should be able to remember more early-night dreams. If you don't write down at least some general notes, you are likely to forget much of the dream or even the entire dream by morning.

Early-night dreams are often more intense. Although I rarely have a nightmare, this is the time of night that I am most likely to have one. Often when I wake up and recall a dream a couple of hours after I go to bed, the dream will feel more intense than a morning dream. It is like the onion analogy. We have several layers. These dreams come from a deeper layer. You will notice that your morning dreams are usually about things that are just beneath the surface. They are things that you probably could sort out consciously given the time to do so. They are the things that you brush aside during the day. The early-night intense dreams are issues that may not have bubbled up to the surface yet. Your brain may be preparing you to start looking at something that you haven't been ready to deal with just yet. These dreams often have very graphic and shocking imagery. They can be violent or sexual. They may contain imagery of death or bizarre symbolism. I believe that these dreams happen earlier in the night intentionally when your mind is best able to handle it. It would be very hard to wake up every day and go to work right after having a shocking dream. This next dream example is a very hard one for me, but I include it in the hopes that my understanding of the meaning can help others.

> *I am in the basement of a house with my children. My children's
> mother is down there too. I hear something upstairs. I realize that
> someone is in the house. I quickly go to grab my children. I grab my
> daughters, but I don't know where my son is. I hope that he finds
> safety. We end up in a laundry room and an evil-looking man comes
> in. My children's mother and I each are hitting this man with sticks
> that look like something I would put in a patio door for security. I can't
> move quickly and I'm hitting him very slow. The scene then changes.
> Police are outside of my childhood home. This man had been arrested,
> but they let him go because they didn't believe he meant any harm. I
> tried to convince them that he really did try to harm us, but nobody
> would listen. The scene changes again. I am outside and I see this man
> in the driveway of a house. He comes up to me carrying a stick like
> the one I hit him with. This one is sharpened at the end. He said that
> he is going to kill me with the same stick that he used on my children.
> I panic and I start to run down the street. I don't see my children's
> mother, but I know that she is ahead of me going toward a house that
> we used to live at. I hear her screaming, "I am so sorry!" I get to the
> house and I see my lifeless children on swings hanging from the maple
> tree. I drop to my knees with my arms out to my sides and let out a
> terrifying shrill.*

I had this dream shortly after I separated from my ex-wife. We were at
the beginning of what turned out to be a very bad divorce. We were arguing
a lot and the children were paying the price for it. I knew better, but my
frustration was sometimes getting the better of me. Communication between
us was terrible. This dream was very graphically trying to show me what this
was doing to our children. It was the most terrifying dream that I have ever
had, but it did serve a purpose. My mind didn't want me participating in that
kind of fighting. Sometimes a shocking dream is necessary in order to get you
to really stop and think about what you are doing, both to yourself and to
other people. Although my divorce continued to be very difficult, I made it a
point to keep the kids away from it as much as I possibly could. I refused to
speak badly about their mother to them or around them. I voluntarily let go
of a lot of things because it wasn't worth the emotional damage to either my
children or me.

Not all intense dreams are nightmares. I would define a nightmare as a
dream that scares me. This next example sounds creepy, but I wasn't frightened
by it. I awoke feeling very intrigued by it.

> *I am in a building. To my right is an interrogation room. The walls are*

cement block and there is a large window looking into the room. As I look into the room, I see a man with a huge head. This head has one eye that is gigantic and it is looking across the table, peering into a little silhouette of a man. As I am watching this, I feel electricity going through my body holding me in place. At the same time, I hear the voice of Hannibal Lecter saying, "He is not like others. He has a need to understand."

The intensity of this dream is matched by only a handful during my lifetime. I felt the physical sense of electricity running through my body as though it was quite real. The imagery was spooky looking, not to mention the voice of Hannibal Lecter.

Hannibal didn't scare me, because I had just watched *The Silence of the Lambs* a couple of days prior. This dream wasn't about serial killers. Hannibal was just the most recent association that I had with psychoanalysts.

I had been working very hard at learning to interpret dreams at this point in my life. It was on my mind a lot, even during the day. Over the previous few weeks, I had become much more successful at my interpretations and I was eager to learn more about myself.

The large eye looking into the little silhouette of a man made an immediate impression on me. I believed the big head with the eye to be a psychoanalyst. It was as though the eye could see directly into the little man.

I remember vividly the words *He is not like others. He has a need to understand.* This was a dream about me looking into my dreams. I was learning a lot of deep things about myself. I believe the dream encouraged this, but was also letting me know that while learning about my own psychology, I may find some things shocking. It was preparing me for the process.

REVIEW
Intense dreams

1. **Keep a pad and paper by the bed.**
   This advice is very common, not only in this book but in numerous others about dreams. But it is perhaps even more important when you are trying to remember more intense dreams. Since they tend to show up earlier in the night, you most likely will forget them if you don't at least jot down some things on paper after you awake from the dream. You won't recall these kinds of dreams as often, so you may want to take advantage of trying to remember then and interpret them when you are able to remember them.

2. **Feel the emotion.**
   Intense dreams may or may not have shocking imagery. Some of them are very graphic, while others just feel more intense. The imagery could be

similar to your other dreams, but your sense of anger, guilt, jealousy, fear, etc. may be heightened. The emotion is the most important aspect of these dreams. At some level, you are not processing that emotion effectively. The dream is bubbling that emotion up to the surface so that you can deal with it. Pretending that it doesn't exist will not help you. Accept that you have those feelings and think about when you experience those emotions in waking life.

CHAPTER 15

Show your fears love and they will go away

Run not one step from the enemy unknown
Lay down your arms, cast not a stone
Risk death to live, surrender to win
It is then that your life will truly begin

One of many lessons that I have learned in my dreams is not to fight against whatever it is that I'm afraid of. Instead I show it love. Keep in mind that the demon in your dream is really a part of you. The angry part of you needs love to heal, not more anger. If you attempt to fight someone or something in your dream, they tend to fight right back. Watch what happens when you show love to your fear.

> *I am in the living room of one of my childhood homes. I hear my father yelling very loudly. He sounds very angry and I am afraid. I try to find him, but I don't know where he is. Now I see him. He is coming down the hallway into the living room. He looks to be about eight feet tall. He looks angry. I realize that this is a dream and I remember that I should try to show him love rather than run away or fight. I walk up to him and hug him. He turns into my childhood dog, who I loved very much.*

Lucid dreams are a good way to put your intentions into practice, but even without a lucid dream you often will act on what you previously intended to do. If you find yourself having dreams about being chased or fighting something, make a conscious decision next time to stop running and stop fighting. Turn around and face whatever "it" is. This sounds hard to do. How can you love some hideous-looking creature that you perceive is trying to hurt you? You *must* remember that this is merely a physical representation of your fears and anxieties. Do not fear these dreams. They are opportunities to heal yourself, and to rid yourself of harmful habits. Show your monster love. Even if you are unable to interpret the meaning of the images, you will still feel that you have healed some part of yourself. Good parents will not hurt their children or run away from them because of a conflict or bad behavior. We may need to correct the behavior, but the love is constant and unconditional. Be that way to yourself. By all means correct behavior that is harmful to yourself or others, but love yourself without condition.

I believe it is best, whenever possible, to handle real-life situations with this same attitude. I am not referring to violent or extreme circumstances, but consider a change of attitude when dealing with more typical situations such as with your family, friends, or coworkers. Minor confrontations are often escalated into something big. We argue with logic but react with emotion. No matter how "right" you may think that you are, at some point you should consider what this is doing to you. Maybe it is better to just let the other person be "right." Have enough confidence in yourself that you don't need validation from others. It is more important to be stress-free, and you never will be if you continue to fight every little thing that comes along. Your other option is to ignore this suggestion and to keep fighting your demons at night. Your higher self wants to be at peace and has no interest in dominating others, verbally or otherwise. Be what you wish others would be, even if they aren't ready to get there yet. At the very least, experiment with this idea in your dreams. I have no doubt that your actions during the day will follow after you feel the healing power of these kinds of dreams.

REVIEW
Show your fears love and they will go away

1. **Note the reactions of your dream demons.**
   Pay attention to how you react to your anger and fears in your dreams. Do you fight those characters? Do you run from them? Do you confront them? Do you try to understand them? What happens after your response? Does the monster fight you back? Does it get angrier? Does it soften and become less scary if you first try to understand it? Do you realize that it is only angry because it is afraid? Remember, you own this dream. You created these characters. They are you. What is it that you need from other people? I'm guessing love and understanding more than fighting and anger.

2. **Practice this attitude in waking life.**

Your dream habits, over time, will mimic your waking habits. If you learn to respond to anger and hatred with kindness and understanding while you are awake, sooner or later that will be your response in your dreams. Whether you are dreaming or awake, reality isn't so different. All of your relationships really take place in your own mind.

CHAPTER 16

Spiritual dreams

Enlighten me to all I see

The storm at night, the sun by day
The black, the white, the shades of gray

The waves, the serenity of a calm sea
Dead branches for firewood, the living tree

The garden flower that smells so sweet
The cigarette butt tossed on the street

The house, the cars, the money I've made
The piles of bills I've left unpaid

Your friends, your family, the people who care
Those whose presence you cannot bear

Are you trapped or are you free?
Enlighten all it is you see

Spiritual dreams can come in many forms. Sometimes it is obvious to you right away and other times you may not realize that the dream was of a spiritual nature until you interpret the dream. My lucid dream about the glowing leaves was one that I knew right away was spiritual. I entitled that dream "Tree of Life." My next example is one that I didn't realize was a spiritual dream until after I understood the meaning of it.

I am driving in a crowded old downtown area near my old college. It is very dark outside. I decide to keep driving past this area and I end up on a winding dirt road. I am following other cars. It becomes pitch black. I cannot see anything at all. I stop the car and open the door. I get out and walk. As I step out of the car, it becomes total daylight. I am next to a mountain. There is a path winding around the mountain leading up. I see blind man with a cane. He is with another man, who is holding on to him and guiding him up the mountain.

I had been going through an emotionally difficult time. I was out of town when I had this dream, and the day prior I had taken a quiet walk along the beach. As I was walking along the beach, I felt a sense of peace despite all my life's circumstances. I recall thinking that getting out and walking always helps me feel better.

The first symbolism that I interpreted in this dream was the phrase *I get out and walk.* I remembered my thoughts from my walk on the beach and made the connection. From there, I was able to understand that I was unable to "see" until I got out and walked. Then I could see. This is telling me literally to get outside and walk, and then I'll be able to see things more clearly. I determined that both the blind man and the guide walking up the mountain were parts of me. The blind man represented the part of me who wasn't able to see, but still wanted to climb to new heights. The guide was the part of me that is always able to see and that would help me get to those new heights. After interpreting this dream, I understood it to mean that my higher self is always guiding me, even when I am unable to see. It left me with a peaceful feeling of knowing that I'm never really alone. Some part of me is always in control and guiding me.

Several months after this dream, I went to the library. I was looking for a specific kind of book in a section that I normally would not be looking in. By chance I saw a book sitting out on a nearby shelf. I don't know why, but I walked over there and picked up the book. The book was about a blind man who climbs mountains. I ended up checking out that book and I enjoyed reading it more than I had enjoyed a book in a long time. It was truly inspiring to me.

Spiritual dreams don't need to be lengthy dreams with elaborate symbols. They can, and often are, the most simple of dreams. In one such case, my entire memory of my dream was that I was holding a business card in my hand. I was reading a book about spiritual signs hours before going to sleep. I had a thought that I would like to receive a sign just letting me know that God or the universe or whatever you choose to call spiritual energy was there with me. Much like in the movie *Oh God* with George Burns, I was holding a business card that simply said, "God." There was my sign.

REVIEW
Spiritual dreams

1. **What makes you feel at peace?**
   Whatever it is that gives you feelings of peace during your waking life will inevitably show up in your dreams. Your unconscious mind wants you to feel good. It doesn't care how much money you have, or how many awards you own. It simply wants you to be at peace. For me, taking a walk often calms my mind and helps me release feelings of stress. Therefore the symbolism of "getting out and walking" has shown up in various dreams. Authors whose work I have found inspirational have shown up in my dreams. You may also find religious or spiritual symbolisms that have meaning for you arriving in your dreams.

2. **Read your verbs.**
   After you write down your dreams, go back and highlight the verbs. Don't worry about the nouns. In my example, I would highlight "I get out and walk." Forget about the car or other symbols. This dream is literally telling me what to do in order to find peace.

3. **Look for simplicity.**
   The answers to finding more peace and spirituality in your life are most likely very simple. It is doubtful that your dreams will suggest that you travel to the other side of the world, climb a mountain, and meditate for forty days and forty nights while chanting. More likely, your dream will suggest something like spending more time in nature, finding more alone time, playing music, or painting.

4. **Watch for premonitions.**
   I have come to realize that virtually all dreams have some premonition involved. In the case of a spiritual dream, I have noticed one slight difference. The time frame for when the premonition manifests itself into reality is often much later. Most of my dream premonitions show up within a few days, but with a spiritual dream it can be months later. These slower premonitions are also of a deeper level than the ones that show up quickly. A premonition that manifests itself within a few days is most likely to be about life's little stresses and issues, whereas a premonition that comes true months later tends to be about finding peace and purpose.

CHAPTER 17

Signs

What is a sign? Is it human or divine?
That depends on how it is your life that you define

Sometimes signs in a dream come literally in the form of a sign. Definitely look for this, because they can be among the easier dreams to interpret. What is a sign to you? To me, it is something that points me in the right direction or tells me something that I need to know. If you think about traffic signs, they tell you when to stop, slow down, use caution, or when there is going to be a bump in the road. A street name may give you a clue to your dream's subject matter. Construction signs may let you know about areas in your life that need work. Arrows may point you in the direction that you need in order to get back on track.

> *I am driving downtown on the highway. There are converging highways, plus exit ramps and smaller streets below and around the highway. The big highways merge in a cloverleaf. I see an exit ramp with a sign that says "Rodeo Street." That ramp is clogged with traffic and I decide not to exit there.*

I often keep a fairly healthy diet, and I try to get exercise regularly. But like many people, I've been known to fall off the wagon from time to time. During the time frame of this dream, I had been sometimes getting a couple of Rodeo Cheeseburgers from Burger King at lunchtime. For me it was convenient, inexpensive, and they tasted good. My dream was telling me that it was time to start looking at other choices.

Having just eaten Rodeo Cheeseburgers for lunch the day before this dream, I made the connection to Rodeo Street quickly. My father had a heart attack and a bypass surgery not long before this. There is a fair amount of heart disease in my family, and I am reaching an age at which I need to start taking that seriously even though my health at the moment is good. In this dream, the highway and other roads represent arteries. If you listen to the morning

72

traffic report, you might even hear the reporter refer to highways as the main arteries. The cloverleaf, smaller roads, and exit ramps were easy for me to see as arteries leading in and out of the heart, especially after having seen images of my dad's heart and arteries not long prior to this. The highways were located downtown, which would indicate the epicenter to me. The exit ramp leading to Rodeo Street was blocked up with traffic. This obviously represents artery blockage.

I had a physical done shortly thereafter, and my health was good. But this dream clearly was a warning to me that I will have problems later if I don't take care of myself now. In the dream, I chose not to exit on Rodeo Street and therefore didn't run into the traffic.

This next example is a dream that I had after getting a prescription for medication to help me with some stress. I had been to the doctor the day before because I had been having some fatigue and stomach problems. The doctor determined that it was all stress-related and she recommended medication to help me relax. I didn't really care for the idea. I prefer more natural methods, such as meditation and exercise. I also wanted to try and resolve some of the issues causing me stress. The doctor agreed, but figured that the medication may help while I was in the process of getting everything else under control.

> *I am going into a nightclub. A band is playing there tonight. I see a big red neon sign that says "Poison." That is the band that is going to be playing here*

Prior to going to sleep, I had hoped that I would have a dream to tell me if the medication was a good idea. Even though this dream sign could not have been clearer, I decided to go ahead and start taking the medication anyway and just see if it would help. This type of medication started with low doses, slowly increasing and building up into my system. I had only been on the medication for about a week when I found that I just wasn't feeling like myself. I was extremely tired and very lethargic. I actually fell asleep one afternoon on the living room floor. The medication did help lower my stress level, but it was because I was so tired that I didn't care about anything other than sleep. The cure was definitely worse than the problem. I spoke to my doctor and we agreed that I should cease usage of the medication. I ended up going back to my original idea of meditation and exercise. It took a bit longer to get my stress level under control, but in the end I was much happier with the result.

REVIEW
Signs

1. **Write down any actual signs that you see in your dream.**
   Signs are a common dream symbolism. Don't overlook them. Traffic

signs are among the most common types. We see traffic signs every day. Their purpose is to guide you in the right direction and prevent accidents. Your signs could also show up as billboards, protest signs, flyers, etc.

2. **What do these signs mean to you?**

    The answer may be something as literal as "Stop!" or "Slow down!" In some cases you will have to give it more thought. In my Rodeo Street example, that street name would not have made much sense to anyone other than me. But it wasn't hard for me to figure out because I had no other recent association with the word *rodeo* other than from the sandwiches that I had been eating.

CHAPTER 18

The body asleep, the mind awake

Between asleep and awake
Past and future
Life and death

…There lies the answer

Dreamlike images that you see as you are falling asleep can be very interesting. Some people fall asleep quickly and have no memory of the process. For me, my consciousness seems to slightly outlast my body. I will see images form as my body falls asleep. The images start out as a stationery photo-type picture, and then begin to move into moving pictures and dreamlike scenes. Some people can induce lucid dreams by falling asleep consciously and keeping their brain awake as their body falls asleep. I definitely believe that anyone can learn to see these images by making an effort to keep their mind focused as their body drifts off. This state of consciousness, halfway between being asleep and awake, is called the hypnagogic state.

I believe that the images in the hypnagogic state are not random. The images or scenes are much the same as in any other dream, and therefore these images can be interpreted. As is the case with lucid dreams, you can be mentally alert while still dreaming. In the hypnagogic state you also may be aware of your physical body, although it is possible that you may lose physical sensation along the way.

The biggest obstacle to interpreting hypnagogic images is simply recalling them. You are likely to have these images in your head as you first fall asleep. After a full night's sleep, you may not recall them. It also is an inconvenient time to wake up to write down the images. I have found that the best way to note down these images is to talk about them as you see them. Sometimes I'll tell my wife what I am seeing as I am falling asleep. When we were dating long-distance, we would talk to each other on the phone late most nights. In the process, one or both of us would sometimes begin to drift off. The phone conversations helped me to keep somewhat alert mentally, but I'd still see these images as my body began to fade. Keeping a tape recorder on the bed may be another way for you to record your hypnagogic images, and in fact some people prefer using a tape recorder to a pen and paper to record all of their dreams.

When my mind is conscious while my body is falling asleep, I prefer not to try to control the images coming into my head. I like to just observe them. I often see things that I consider to be beautiful, like a close-up of a flower or a child playing with a puppy. My interpretation of these kinds of images is that my mind is calming my thoughts to help prepare me for a good night's rest. Here and there I will see an image that reminds me of something that I want to do, as though my mind is putting that thought on the back burner so that I'll be more likely to remember to do some task the following day.

I have noticed some very strange occurrences during the hypnagogic state. I'll provide some examples and suggest that you experiment with your own images. These examples are things that I told my wife when we were dating and making late-night long-distance calls.

> • *I see a stain on your living room floor. It is right behind the left rear leg of your computer chair. The stain is about the size of a silver dollar. There is something white and fuzzy on the stain, with just a little bit of red in the white fuzzy part.*

I hadn't been to my wife's former house in several days. She insisted that there was no stain on the carpet, but curiosity got the better of her. As you can probably guess, there was a fresh stain on her living room carpet behind the left rear leg of her computer chair. The dog had gotten hold of a marker. There was also a piece of white fluff on the stain that even included a small red fuzzy part.

> • *I see a single slice of sausage pizza.*

After telling my wife that I was seeing one slice of sausage pizza, she told me that she had gone out for a walk earlier that day and stopped into the local pizza shop. She picked up one slice of sausage pizza to eat as she walked.

> • *I see an angel looking down over your house.*

My wife had been cleaning the house. She moved a bookshelf to vacuum and she found a lace Christmas angel that had fallen behind it. The angel had been missing for months. She hung it up on the wall right over her bed, and mentioned it to me after I told her about my angel image.

As you continue to fall asleep, the hypnagogic images become more like normal dreams. Slowly the photographs turn into moving pictures. Initially I see them like I am looking at a movie screen, but as the scenes begin to move I become a part of that scene. Eventually they lead right into regular dreams, which explains why I can wake up and remember a dream shortly after I have gone to bed.

There are other kinds of nighttime experiences that people have reported that do not seem to fit under the description of being a dream or dreamlike. I have recalled thousands of dreams during my lifetime ranging from pleasant to nightmares. I have had lucid dreams, premeditative dreams, and of course many "average" dreams. The one thing that they all have in common is that I can safely refer to them all as dreams. Even the imagery that I see as I fall asleep is simply the earliest stage of a dream. For all my lifetime of dream experiences, I have had exactly one that does not fit my understanding of what a dream is. I was eighteen years old and remember it as though it was last night.

I am lying down on my bed late at night looking around my room. The blinds are slightly opened and I can see a nearly full moon shining into my room giving it some light. I see my posters on the walls and some furniture lit by the moonlight. I hear something that catches me off guard. I hear snoring, and I realize that it is coming from me. I then realize that I have no sensation of my body. My body is fully asleep, yet here I am totally awake and conscious. My reaction to this is fear. I'm not sure what to think and I have this thought that something scary is going to happen. As soon as I have this thought, I see a large glowing skull appear on my wall. I realize that it was my own thought that created this, and the skull disappears. My next thought is that I want to be someplace that I feel safe. Instantly I am in my parents' living room. It is dark there too, but the moonlight is shining somewhat in from the living room window. I move around the living room and into the dining room where I see a bunch of paperwork of my mom's on the dining room table. I start to go down the hallway to look in on my parents, but then feel that it is too scary and I don't want to see them. Instead I decide to start looking around the room to find something that can prove to myself that this is real. I want to find something that I wouldn't otherwise know about and then confirm it the following day. I start to look at the dining room table, but then think that Mom may move some of those papers in the morning. I go in front of the living room window and look at the plants. One of them catches my attention because it has a couple of leaves that are half alive and half dead. I crouch down by it and take a very close look at some specific markings

> *that I would never have noticed or even bothered to pay any attention to. After looking for several seconds, I step right through the living room window and I am now floating in the air. I start to rise and I am now looking down over the house and trees. I am afraid and I don't understand what is happening. I am wondering if I am dead and how that could be. I think, "I want to be back in my body" and instantly awoke in my room. The time was a few minutes after two AM.*

I have had my share of intense and spiritual dreams, but this was not like them. Every dream that I can recall—and I mean every one of the thousands of them—has had a few things in common. The places that I am in the dream are not exactly as they are in real life. My home, for example, in a dream may look very similar to my real-life home or it could be totally different. But never is it identical. In this case, my room as well as my parents' house had absolutely no difference from waking life to real life. The posters were in the right places, the plants, the table and the paperwork on the table, the furniture, the size and color of the rooms themselves. Even the moonlight shining into my room was accurate. Dream imagery also changes. In any other dream, if I were to look at a poster or a plant, they would not stay looking the same. Dreams don't have the ability to hold an image steady. In fact in any other dream if I looked at one of the posters, then looked away and looked back, it would have changed to something entirely different. That didn't happen here. Everything stayed stationary. So did I have an out-of-body experience or is it possible that I had a dream with a level of realness unlike anything I have ever experienced? In either case, there are many possibilities of where we can go with our minds.

REVIEW
The body asleep, the mind awake

1. **Talk to your partner or use a tape recorder.**
   Chances are that you won't remember the images that you see as you are falling asleep, unless you somehow record them. You won't get a good night's sleep if you keep waking yourself up to write them down. Eventually you need to let yourself drift off. However, talking as you are drifting off doesn't seem to prevent you from falling asleep.
2. **Observe.**
   These images have been very interesting and strange at times for me. I have found it most enjoyable not to try and shape the images, but simply let them become what they will. Even as I see these images, I sometimes think, "I wonder why I'm seeing that?"
3. **Watch for unusual coincidences.**
   For reasons that I do not understand, these images seem to include a high percentage of coincidences. My only thought on this is that perhaps in a

quieted state of mind, we become more receptive to signals from outside of ourselves. If you are not consciously controlling the images, then where do they come from and why?

4. **Understand what makes a dream a dream.**

   If you have an unusual experience, write it down and share it with someone that you trust, and I welcome you to write to me about this. I am interested in learning about unique nighttime experiences.

CHAPTER 19

Dream sex

Think if you will that your life is concealed
Then open your eyes and see it revealed

Most sexual dreams are not about sex at all. Although that may not be true one hundred percent of the time, the sexual content of dreams is there to trigger a strong emotion. Sex is a topic that people are often uncomfortable with at one level or another. Sexual dreams often involve situations or people that you would definitely not participate with in real life. That often invokes feelings of inappropriateness, shock, disgust, discomfort, and fear. The dream is really about those feelings. Sexual content is there to bring out those emotions on a strong, even shocking level. That can occur whether you are physically participating, involved in a conversation about the topic, or observing others.

> *I am downstairs. My parents are upstairs arguing about sex. I hear my mom mention something about clothing used as some kind of role-playing thing between them. I hear her use the word sex as she is yelling at my dad. I do not want to hear this. Mom comes downstairs. I grab her arm and pull her aside. I want to tell her that I don't want to hear that. Now it is my son that is with me. I tell him that it is not okay for his grandparents to be arguing like that. I don't want him to hear that.*

This dream is about concerns that I had for my son. He had been telling me that his mother and her boyfriend had been getting into a lot of arguments. He seemed sad when he told me this. He didn't want to be around that. Worse yet, it reminded him of arguments that his mother and I had when we were together.

The concept of my parents arguing about sex can be seen in the phrase *I do not want to hear this.* Hearing a conversation about sex between my parents would indeed make me quite uncomfortable. I heard my parents argue quite a bit when I was a child, and it made me very uncomfortable. My concerns for my son hearing arguments were portrayed by my own memories of hearing my parents argue. I ended up telling my son in the dream that I don't want him to hear that. The reason that my parents were arguing about sex is because of the degree of discomfort that it created in the dream. If my parents were arguing about something else, it would not have had the same level of shock and discomfort.

Frequently you are the person who is participating on a physical level. These can be among the most difficult kinds of dreams to share with someone else. Even though it is just a dream, you may still have the natural feelings of embarrassment or need for privacy. Worse yet, if your significant other has not studied dream interpretation, that person may assume that your sexual dream with someone else is a fantasy. Rarely is that the case, and I will provide examples to help you clarify what these dreams might really be saying to you.

I am in the bedroom of my first house. It looks like it did back then. My ex-wife is there and it is as though we are still married. She wants to have sex. I do not want to, but she is aggressive and I give in. She quickly satisfies her own needs, then gets up and leaves the room. I then notice that she has a bunch of new expensive clothes, purses, and shoes by the wall across the room.

This dream occurred during the early stages of my divorce. I had been feeling taken advantage of financially. I was hoping not to have to fight it out in court, but eventually I had to accept that is where things were headed. The key ideas that I noticed were that she was being aggressive, and that I gave in. She also satisfied her own needs with no concern for mine. That definitely describes my feelings at the time. The expensive items that she had was fairly direct about how I felt that the money I had been giving her was being used. So again the question comes up, Why is sex involved in this dream? If the dream had simply been about having an argument with my ex-wife, I probably would not have paid much attention to the dream. My ex-wife and I were arguing frequently at that time and the dream would have been little different from waking life. I woke up from this dream feeling very uncomfortable, and that was the point. Emotions create change in our lives, even the emotions that aren't pleasant. A change needed to be made for the overall betterment of my life. I needed to feel that discomfort.

Even fantasy-related sexual dreams are often more emotional than physical. During my first marriage, I was often unhappy with my relationship and felt like a lot was missing. I had several dreams much like the following one.

I am in a house with a girl that I like. She is very pretty, although I can't really make out her face. I know that she likes me too. I feel a sense of love in a way that I haven't felt in a very long time. We don't say anything. We kiss and I enjoy it. I am hoping for more. She has to leave the room. I go to look for her, but I can't find her.

In this dream, I am trying to feel and experience something that I wasn't feeling in real life. That is why I was unable to find the girl. In several of these dreams, I never remembered a face. Even though there were some sexual overtones in this dream, it was more about feelings than sex. Once I came to the conclusion that I wanted a divorce, these dreams abruptly stopped.

True sexual fantasy dreams can happen, although I believe they are in the minority of sexual dreams. People who suppress their sexual urges, perhaps because of religious or moral beliefs, may release some of those feelings in dreams. However, that doesn't mean that every sexual dream that a conservative person has is a fantasy. Most are probably related to their discomfort with the topic of sex, their moral beliefs, or their feelings about sin. For someone with strong convictions on the subject, sex can be a powerful symbol for stirring their emotions.

I believe the most common type of actual sexual fantasy dream to be one in which the person is aware of what they are doing, such as in a lucid dream. Sex in lucid dreams is very common, and actions in lucid dreams are often more literal than standard dreams.

One way that you can differentiate between a sexual fantasy dream and a sexual symbolism dream is, frankly, how good the sex is. In dreams where sex is a symbol for something else, generally your emotions in the dream will not be very positive. You feel uncomfortable, used, or fearful. The other person or people involved very likely are not people you would ever have a fantasy about, much less actually have sex with. In a sexual fantasy dream, the experience is enjoyable. Keep in mind, however, that a positive sexual dream also may very well not be truly about sex. Feelings of enjoyment, satisfaction, love, or other positive emotions might be related to something else in your life indicating that you are on the right path. Once again, it all comes down to emotions.

REVIEW
Dream sex

1. **Notice your emotions.**
   More often than not, sex in dreams is used as a symbolism to trigger an emotion. The emotion that you feel in the dream will tell you much about what this dream is really saying to you. Feelings of discomfort, inappropriateness, disgust, fear of being caught, etc. are what you should be looking for. Sex is merely the symbolism to bring those emotions to the surface. Positive feelings may tell you that you are doing something right, including feelings of satisfaction and pleasure.

2.   Remove the nouns.

After having a sexual dream people often focus on the act of sex and end up misinterpreting the dream. In addition to focusing on the feelings, you can also find out what these dreams mean by removing the nouns from your sentences and focusing on the verbs. For example, in the dream with my ex-wife I would narrow the sentences down as follows: She wants to. I do not want to. She is aggressive. I give in. She satisfies her own needs. By removing the nouns, I can forget about the sexual content of the dream and focus on the actions using very basic words.

CHAPTER 20

Physical health dreams

If my body were my child
I would feed it well
And exercise it with play

If my body were my child
I would encourage it to always to do its best
But let it rest when it needed it

If my body were my child
I would never let anyone harm it
And I would love it without condition

Physical health dreams can show up in a variety of different ways. We have already seen an example with my Rodeo Street dream pointing out that I am risking blocked arteries by not keeping a healthier diet. Fast-food restaurants often show up in my dreams when my diet needs adjusting. If you smoke, drink, or have other habits that can affect your health, perhaps you will find symbolism that you can associate. Maybe a sign that you need more exercise will show up as you having trouble running or walking in a dream. One evening after having a couple of drinks, I had the following dream.

I am looking in the mirror. My neck is long and made of a clear plastic tube. I see fish rotting in there.

My daughter had recently purchased a goldfish. The water in the fishbowl often had to be changed, or it became cloudy and could become unhealthy for the fish. The clear plastic of my neck was similar to the material that the goldfish bowl was made of. Essentially this dream was telling me to find a better way to relax than by having a drink.

It is no secret that stress can create physical symptoms. You might be surprised at the healing power of dreams, particularly when stress is the culprit.

> *I am in a machine shop. I see a large plastic tube. Other people in*
> *the room also each have one of these. Mine is all bent up. People are*
> *feeding their tubes through a machine that cleans out their tubes, but I*
> *can't because mine is bent. I grab each end of the tube and I am able*
> *to pull it mostly straight. I can now feed it through the machine and it*
> *comes out clean.*

I had been having some stomach and intestinal problems as a result of stress. After this dream, those problems seemed to end. I still had some stress issues to deal with, but I felt like I was no longer holding that stress in my stomach and intestines.

Pay attention to the inner workings of your house within a dream. The bulk of your house is related to your emotions, but certain parts tend to be about your physical self. This would include things like running water, electricity, plumbing, heating and air-conditioning, and appliances. The next example was an elaborate dream mostly unrelated to my physical health, but there was a small piece of the dream that was.

> *I am in my house, which is quite large. There is a lot of company*
> *visiting and the air-conditioning is not working properly. I go upstairs*
> *to check the thermostat. First I flip a light switch on, but the lights*
> *aren't working right either. They are flickering, like there is a short*
> *somewhere. Eventually the air-conditioning kicks in, but I realize that*
> *it is in need of repair.*

I had this dream shortly before finding out that a herniated disc in my neck was the culprit of some physical pain and discomfort. The disc was pinching a nerve, and as time went on I began to have a lot of numbness down my left arm. Other symptoms included muscle spasms and a feeling of heat in my chest. The flickering lights I believed in the dream were caused by a short are representative of the pinched nerve. The feeling of heat in my chest shows up as the air-conditioning not working properly. I ended up needing surgery to repair this problem, and it is clear that my mind was aware of this in advance of me getting medical confirmation.

REVIEW
Physical health dreams

1. Find your associations.
At first glance it can be difficult to tell when your dream is about physical

health issues, versus emotional health. Over time, I have learned to recognize certain associations that I have with certain symbols or words. To me, fast-food restaurants are something that I associate with being physically unhealthy. On the other hand, fruits and vegetables are something that I see as being healthy choices.

2. **Objects can represent parts of your body.**

    Any number of objects can show up in your dreams representing body parts. In this book, I have already used examples of highways representing arteries and a plastic tube representing intestines. I have also seen such things as car tires representing feet or legs, and an airplane wing representing my arm. If you have an ailment that has been bothering you, pay close attention to the objects in your dream. If your left arm is hurting and you have a dream in which an airplane or a bird has a broken wing, I'd bet that it is the left wing. The key to this dream, of course, is to see what you do to fix it.

CHAPTER 21

Travel dreams

This path that I walk will look different to my children
Because the trees that I planted along the way will have grown

With some luck, those trees will provide them with shade
And give them a place to climb where they can see things that I never could

Travel dreams are very common. You may be traveling by car, airplane, bike, boat, train, or on foot. Regardless of your medium of travel, you are attempting to get from one place to another. Chances are, you either get lost or you forget something. Sometimes you have trouble seeing as you are driving, or you run into bad weather or some kind of obstacle that prevents you from getting to where you want to go. These dreams often include feelings of stress, frustration, or anxiety. Traveling from one place to another is a metaphor for trying to get someplace emotionally, or trying to reach a goal.

I am trying to drive to my old house. I can't get there. The old roads
have all been ripped up and new ones are being paved. I don't know
my way around the neighborhood anymore.

This dream occurred after my ex-wife and I had separated. I was living in an apartment at the time, unsure of where my life was headed in many ways. I didn't know how often I would be able to see my kids, where I would be living, or what my financial situation would be. The old roads having been ripped up and new ones being paved is a metaphor that is easy to understand.

My dad and I are supposed to be bringing my son to the airport. Dad
isn't home yet and I realize that we are running very late. I am about
to leave when Dad gets home. He wants to drive. We are having a hard
time finding our way to the airport. We keep going around the highway
in a loop. I know there is a road near here that leads to the airport,

but we can't find it. Dad doesn't want to ask for directions. We end up on foot in a shopping mall. I decide to run ahead through hallways to find the airport. I run quickly, weaving in and out of people. There is a fork where the hallway splits into two separate hallways. I choose the right side and I end up by the airport. I realize that I already have my son's ticket in my shirt pocket, so we can save time by not having to buy him the ticket. There are security guards in front of the airport, but they aren't doing much. I ask if this is the airport and one security guard sarcastically responds yes, as though it should be obvious to me. I run back to go get my son, but now the hall is angled uphill and I'm having trouble running back to get him. It takes a lot of effort.

I had some concerns about my son at this time. I am trying desperately to get him someplace before it is too late. My dad driving represents the father in me taking over control. His refusal to ask for directions is indicative of me trying too hard to do it all on my own. Perhaps I need some help. Security guards show up in my dreams from time to time. They represent the word *security.* I start out by going around the same highway loop several times, which means I am repeating some habit or pattern. Eventually I do find my way— and in fact I choose the "right" hallway—but then I have trouble getting back to my son. This means that I can figure out what to do easier than I can get myself to do it. It is going to take a lot of effort.

REVIEW
Travel dreams

1. **Understand the metaphor.**
   Travel dreams very rarely are about physically getting from one place to another. They are about trying to get someplace emotionally or about reaching a goal. If you are having trouble making it to your destination, realize that this really means that you are having trouble achieving your goal or getting past a problem.

2. **What is in your way?**
   Paying attention to what is in your way will provide you with additional details to make a proper interpretation. Perhaps you *forgot* the car keys, or you *can't see* through the windshield. There could be *too many* obstacles in your way, you don't know how to fly the plane, or the train *has already left and you are too late.*

CHAPTER 22

Death dreams

A whisper separates life from death
For it only takes one breath
And when your breath has reached its end
That whisper to another send

People often fear death dreams. Some believe that death in a dream means death in real life. I can assure you that I have physically survived several deaths in my dreams. Death is another symbol that creates strong feelings. There is a fear of the unknown. Death can represent change or transformation. A dream death can be a positive or negative experience. In either case, the message is usually a strong one. What happens after you die in your dream will give you many clues to the dream's real meaning. Did you go to heaven? Did you go to hell? Were you reincarnated? Was their pain? Did you see previously deceased friends or relatives?

> *I am in some kind of crypt. It is dark, although I can see. It is musty and unpleasant. This place is entirely enclosed with concrete. Someone is in there now. They shoot me in the chest. The world around me fades. I fall to the ground and everything goes black. I know that I am dead. I see and feel nothing, but my consciousness is still there. I am afraid that I am trapped in this void.*

I had this dream many years ago. I recall asking myself, "What does this crypt remind me of?" I thought of cramped, dark, dreary places and realized that this described my feeling of the office that I was working in. There were no windows and it was rather cramped in there. I really disliked the working environment. Besides the physical environment, I was also dealing with a lot of job stress at the time. I felt trapped. I didn't feel like I could cut it financially if I left for something else. Also, this was a family business and I felt a lot of obligation to tough it out. My death in the dream and being stuck in the "void" represented my fear of not finding happiness in my working environment. I was trapped, conscious of what was going on around me, but feeling powerless to do anything. This dream was all about telling me how badly my job stress was affecting me. The symbolism of being shot in the chest and spending eternity in a dark void was strong, and led me to make changes. Although I stuck with this job, my dad and I agreed that we should move the business. We moved to a nicer building and I got my own small office with a window. We also let go of a problem employee and made some other decisions that significantly improved the working environment. Although not necessarily my dream job (no pun intended), I was able to see that something had to be done to make some immediate changes in my job environment in order to cut down on stress, and the improvements were significant.

The feelings were more uplifting in another death dream...

> *I am in the downstairs family room. I hear a loud rumble and realize that there is a tornado. I feel the house lift up. I sense the feeling of the house falling back down to the ground. As the houses crashes, everything goes black. I open my eyes and realize that I have died. There is an old man with white hair and a long white beard standing over me. I see rubble all over the place, but the sky is now sunny. I get up and look around. I know that I have been reincarnated, although physically I feel the same. I find a mirror and look at my face. I look mostly the same, except a bit older.*

I had this dream about the time that I had graduated high school. Death was symbolic of a major change in my life. Reincarnation represented entering a new life, as can also be seen in the symbolism of being older in my reflection in the mirror. My house crashing, and the rubble, represented my old life being gone. The sunny skies showed me that things were looking good on the horizon. The old man with the long white beard represented the part of me that is wisdom.

REVIEW
Death dreams

1. **Has there been a major change in your life?**
    Death represents finality and "crossing over" into new territory. Whether it is a positive or negative situation, change can create very strong feelings. Some life experiences that could bring about death dreams could be getting married, getting divorced, having a baby, the actual death of a family member or friend, graduation, moving, or a new job. If you have had a major change in your life, consider that a death dream may simply be representing the ending of something—and along with that the start of something new.

2. **Describe the physical or emotional feelings during your death.**
   The words that you use to describe your death in the dream will tell you most of what you need to know. Some common feelings could be pain, peace, fear, or acceptance. Death is a strong symbolism. Chances are the feelings that you are sorting out are also strong.

CHAPTER 23

Dissecting your dreams

Drop of rain, journey home
Travel with storm clouds
Trust the wind
You will fall from the sky
And be picked up by the river
The river will be rough at times
But trust its path
It shall return you to the ocean

One of the reasons dreams can be so difficult to interpret is that they are often lengthy and detailed. Sometimes it is almost overwhelming. If you wake up remembering some elaborate lengthy dream, initially it can seem almost impossible to find the true meaning behind many changing symbols. One of the methods that I have used to work around that problem is to break down the dream into smaller parts. Dreams have scenes, much like movies or television shows. You may see a television show, such as a soap opera, that contains several story lines at once. Even though you are watching only one show, in many ways you are watching several stories at one time. Dreams are much the same. I'll give an example here of a lengthy and detailed dream, then show how it can be broken down to make more sense of it.

I am walking in a newer housing development. The development
follows a circular pattern, perhaps around a lake. There are a lot of
people walking along the road or pathway. It seems like there should be
a lot of traffic in this area, yet it is very nice. One house in particular
is set a bit higher than the rest. It isn't quite completed. It is very nice
with a brick exterior and a concrete driveway. Even though there is a

lot of traffic in front of it, although it seems like foot traffic, I think it has the nicest lot. I now am walking elsewhere in an area that looks at first to be outdoors, then indoors. It is also nice, but not as nice as the other development. These developments are connected, like they are located close to each other. It is like one is a bit older than the other, but that they were built by the same people. I see on my left a large building with nice windows on it. It seems to be housing, but more like community housing than a single-family home. It then seems like it was built around an indoor rectangular pool. I talk to my friend Frank and tell him that this place, the older place, has its own movie theaters and a bar, as though I am trying to make him think that I am living in a nice place. I even think or say that the movie theaters are small. I am now in a buffet line, like at a cafeteria. There is a guy there who is talking to me and some other people. He is a nice guy and is the person who mainly is directing the conversation. I put breakfast food on my plate, specifically cheese eggs. I have some trouble getting just the right amount on my plate. The eggs are sticking a little bit to the serving spoon. Either I or another other guy drops his fork on the floor and has to get a new one. There is music playing, like it is a theme to this place. I think that the people working here must get tired of hearing the same thing over and over. But at the same time I figure that they just get used to it knowing that it makes a nice atmosphere for the customers.

Separating this dream into different scenes made it much easier for me to understand the meaning. If you look in the beginning sentences, you can see where the scene changes.

*I am walking in a newer housing development. The development follows a circular pattern, perhaps around a lake. There are a lot of people walking along the road or pathway. It seems like there should be a lot of traffic in this area, yet it is very nice. One house in particular is set a bit higher than the rest. It isn't quite completed. It is very nice with a brick exterior and a concrete driveway. Even though there is a lot of traffic in front of it, although it seems like foot traffic, I think it has the nicest lot. **I now am walking elsewhere in an area that looks at first to be outdoors, then indoors.***

The section of the dream in which I am walking in a newer housing development comes to an end. The scenery now shifts to where I am walking elsewhere. By sectioning out the first scene, I have fewer words and images to sort through. Here is what I came up with.

I had been questioning what might be some good ideas to improve my work life. I had been working some with candy machines, and I had also considered some other options. The circular pattern of the development in my dream represents a route—my candy-machine route. Foot traffic is very important in being successful with candy machines, so the fact that this is a nice neighborhood with a lot of foot traffic indicates that there is a lot of merit to this candy-machine idea. The one house—a very nice one—isn't yet completed. This home had the nicest lot. I only had a handful of candy machines. This part of the dream was telling me that increasing my route would be a good business idea.

Now let's take a look at the next scene…

> *I now am walking elsewhere in an area that looks at first to be outdoors, then indoors. It is also nice, but not as nice as the other development. These developments are connected, like they are located close to each other. It is like one is a bit older than the other, but that they were built by the same people. I see on my left a large building with nice windows on it. It seems to be housing, but more like community housing than a single-family home. It then seems like it was built around an indoor rectangular pool. I talk to my friend Frank and tell him that this place, the older place, has its own movie theaters and a bar, as though I am trying to make him think that I am living in a nice place. I even think or say that the movie theaters are small.* **I am now in a buffet line, like at a cafeteria.**

I thought about what the scenery was like. In many ways it sounded like the office building that I was working at with my family's business. We had an office suite in a building with many other businesses, which explains the community housing. My friend Frank used to work with me at this business. Frank now successfully runs his own business, and he is someone whose business ideas I respect. This place is older, but also nice. It isn't as nice as the other place, and I try to convince Frank that it is nicer than it really is. My emotions in the dream matched up with emotions in real life about how I felt with this job. It had its good points, but I often spoke more highly of it than I felt. I had also spoken to my wife the night before about how the job was more fun for me when Frank was working there. I had more social interaction. The movie theater and bar is a representation of fun and social interaction. The two developments in the dream are connected, which makes sense because I am heavily involved in both businesses.

After this, I move into a seemingly unrelated scene in a cafeteria…

> *I am now in a buffet line, like at a cafeteria. There is a guy there who is talking to me and some other people. He is a nice guy and is the person who mainly is directing the conversation. I put breakfast food on my plate, specifically cheese eggs. I have some trouble getting just the right*

amount on my plate. The eggs are sticking a little bit to the serving spoon. Either I or some other guy drops his fork on the floor and has to get a new one. There is music playing, like it is a theme to this place. I think that the people working here must get tired of hearing the same thing over and over. But at the same time I figure that they just get used to it knowing that it makes a nice atmosphere for the customers.

Restaurants are common in my dreams. The type of restaurant has a lot of meaning. Consider your own associations with family restaurants, cafeterias, fast food, or expensive restaurants. To me, a cafeteria represents choices. Another association that I have with the word *cafeteria* is related to a benefit plan we had at the family business. We had sometimes referred to it as a "cafeteria plan." This portion of the dream continues the subject of business choices. When I consider the symbolism of eggs getting stuck on a serving spoon and having difficulty getting the right amount on my plate, I see this as meaning that I'm having trouble getting unstuck in some area and determining how much I should be doing. I mention that this restaurant has music playing over and over again, and that the employees get used to it knowing that it makes a nice atmosphere for the customers. This represents that, although I may be bored doing the same thing day after day, I can take some pride in knowing that I am doing some work that is appreciated by others.

The night prior to having this dream, I had asked myself to have a dream that would help me with my career. My mind came up with a combination of different things that I could do right now to help move things in the right direction. First, the candy machines provided me with an opportunity that I would see as most attractive. Second, I could make my existing job at the family business a more positive place to work mainly by simply adjusting my attitude. I might be bored, but I could still have pride in my work.

The part about dropping the fork on the floor didn't make sense until after I had a conversation with my secretary several hours after I awoke from this dream. She was talking to me about her current husband and mentioned something odd about her late husband along the way. She said that her late husband often liked to have things done in certain ways and she gave me an example. She had to learn that certain forks were used for certain things, like having a separate fork for a salad. She said that now she uses whatever fork that she wants to use. The fork symbolism now fit into my dream. This whole dream was about choices at work. My secretary is certainly someone that I associate with work. I am being told that I don't have to do things a certain way out of some family obligation. I can choose to "use whatever fork" that I want to.

REVIEW

Dissecting your dreams

1. **Look for the scene change.**

   Long dreams can be way too confusing to try to figure it out by reading back through the entire dream. But you should be able to see where the dream changes scenes. Think of each new scene as a new dream. After I type my dreams into my computer, I will sometimes actually cut out a dream scene and paste it onto a clean page. That helps me to focus on a much smaller portion of the dream.

2. **Find the common connection.**

   Even though I may separate my dream out into a few "minidreams," remember that it is still one dream. Therefore, the subject matter of the various scenes will be related. In my example, it was about my career. The scenes showed me different areas of my work life, and perhaps even some different options. Once I had come to the realization that this dream was helping me with some career decisions, I was able to look for symbolisms related to that area of my life in each of the scenes.

CHAPTER 24

Your dream house

Electric lights may mimic day
But candle flame will light my way

Your house in a dream most likely represents you. Someone else's house may not, but if you know the dream to be your own house, notice how the various rooms represent various parts of your personality. Even if the house doesn't look like your house, you still will know in the dream if it is supposedly yours.

> *I am in my house. The house is very big. I am in the kitchen, which looks a lot like my former in-laws' kitchen. I see through the kitchen across a hallway. There is a room across the hallway that looks a lot like my office. The carpet is the same and I see a desk. I walk upstairs and it is a school up there. The hallway is long and I see classrooms on either side. I see one teacher outside of a classroom. I go back downstairs all the way to the basement. The basement is cluttered. I see that there is a cellar door in the basement. I open it and it leads to a deeper basement. There is a ladder that goes down there. It is a single room, about the size of a small bedroom. There is nothing in there. The walls are cement block and the floor is concrete. There is a single lightbulb hanging from the ceiling. It is clean in there. I thought about going down there, but I changed my mind. I know that something bad happened down there. Even though there is nothing down there now, I'd still rather not go down.*

In most dreams, the house is the scenery with many other things going on in the dream. In this example, the house is the centerpiece of the entire dream. It represents various parts of my life, both current and past as seen by the kitchen looking like my former in-laws' and my office being a part of it. Upper levels in my dreams are almost always educational or spiritual. In this case it was a school, representing higher learning. The basement being cluttered is also common in my dreams. Basements in dreams are often musty, cluttered, and filled with many things from both your present and past. It is where you store things. In this case, there was an even deeper basement, symbolizing yet a deeper level of my consciousness. There is some aspect of my personality, or some memories, that I wasn't ready to deal with on a conscious level at that time. Dreams have a way of slowly bubbling those kinds of things to the surface.

REVIEW
Your dream house

1. **Your house represents your mind and body.**
   In most dreams, a house that is yours (or that you know to be yours in the dream) is not just scenery. A house is where you live. If you pay close attention to your dream houses, you will see various aspects of your life, personality, and body. Your physical body could be represented in things such as the electrical wiring, plumbing, and appliances. The rooms will have different meanings depending on your personal associations. Generally, the basement represents the "lower" part of yourself or a storage area, whereas the upper levels can be educational or spiritual in nature. Notice if the rooms remind you of other places, or if there are extra rooms that normally wouldn't be there.
2. **Notice the big rooms.**
   Your entire dream house will probably be much bigger than your real house, but notice any room or rooms in particular that are larger than normal. Any large items in dreams are there to call your attention to it. If the kitchen is very big, then notice what is in the kitchen. Does this kitchen remind you of someplace? Is the kitchen being used? Is it clean or dirty? What kind of appliances is there? How do you feel in this room?
3. **Look at the carpeting.**
   I have often found a connection to a place in a dream by the carpeting. Sometimes I have no initial recognition of a room that I'm in, but when I give further thought to the carpet I'll realize that it looks like my office carpeting or the carpeting from a childhood home. You may find the same to be true with wallpaper or paint, curtains, appliances, or various other objects within the house.

CHAPTER 25

Construction and remodeling

I will build it, though it will crumble
For it is made just for the humble
And it will last for the time they need
To plant the rubble as a new seed

Construction and remodeling are common themes in dreams. Although they can be the main focus of your dream, often they are a more subtle part of the background. Even so, the construction may—literally—be the foundation on which the rest of the dream is built.

> *I am in the basement of a house that is under construction. I believe this to be Mom and Dad's house. Chris and the kids are there. I put clothes in the wash and I suggest to Chris that I run to McDonald's to get some food for us and the kids while the clothes are washing. I try taking orders, but everyone is talking at once and I am getting frustrated. I have trouble remembering what everyone wants.*

I had this dream shortly after my wife and I had moved in together and blended our families. We were in the early stages of developing our new household routines and adjusting to being a family of six. The construction represented something new being built. The fact that this was my parents' house meant that the words *Mom* and *Dad* were a key element. The basement in this case represented the bottom floor, or the foundation, on which everything else was being built. One of the things that we noticed quickly after blending our families is how much laundry we were doing. It seemed that the amount of chores overall were more than expected, but laundry was a good symbolism for me. Suggesting that I go to McDonald's was a way of trying to figure out how to get more done at once by finding convenience. I end up taking everyone's order, but I have trouble remembering what everyone wants and I get frustrated. This shows some frustration that I was having in adjusting to our new family routines. I was having trouble figuring out what everyone wanted.

The construction was a key in this dream, because it showed that things were still being built. Although I was frustrated, the development process was still underway. If this dream had taken place in an older home where there was no construction or remodeling occurring, it may have meant that the frustration was a more permanent fixture.

REVIEW
Construction and remodeling

1. **Construction is something new.**
   If there is new construction in your dream, it represents something new in your life. It could be a new relationship, a new job, or perhaps moving into a new neighborhood. Consider any areas of your life in which something is new, and most likely still in the process of being developed. That is the foundation, or key subject matter, of your dream.

2. **Remodeling is changing something that is already there.**
   In a remodeling dream, you might be putting in new carpet, adding rooms, or even demolishing something that you already own. The place that this occurs may give you some clue, such as if the dream occurs at your place of work. The process of remodeling shows that the basic foundation is still intact, but changes may be necessary or may be already in progress. Rather than finding a new relationship, the one you are involved in currently may be different somehow. Maybe you still work at the same place, but you are up for a promotion. Definitely pay attention to whether or not the construction in your dream is building something new or remodeling something that is already there.

CHAPTER 26

Run-down buildings

The antique from generations past
Of modern styles will always outlast
And though the trendy is grand today
Before generation next it shall decay

The opposite of construction is buildings that are being demolished or are deteriorating. These images can show you areas in your life that are being neglected. Sometimes run-down buildings can symbolize the physical or emotional feelings of being run-down. In other cases, these dreams may represent that something doesn't look as good or is not working out as well as you would like. Pay attention to the details. In some cases the building may be old, but the construction is still sound. Maybe it just needs a renovation or cleaning. In other cases the building should be torn down completely.

Chris and I are out of town. The hotels in the area are like ones that we've stayed at before, but they seem run-down. They are old and have not been well maintained. My memories of these hotels are nicer than what I am seeing.

We had been attempting to plan both a honeymoon and a family vacation during the summer. I had a lot of grand ideas of fun things to do and places we could go. Unfortunately we ran into various snags. I had difficulty working out a summer schedule with my ex-wife. My wife was unable to get time off work during the weeks that we had wanted. I ended up having to give up on the plans that I had hoped for. I was very disappointed.

The hotels in my dream were ones in which my wife and I had previously stayed at. My memories of them were good, but they were looking run-down and not well maintained. This symbolizes my feelings of reality not matching up with my vision.

The good news is that dreams are there to help you. Rather than just pointing out that I am disappointed, subsequent dreams gave me ideas on other things that I could do in order to still have fun. In the end, we had only one week to work with so we made the best of it. We took the kids with us for half of the trip and were alone for the second half. I needed to refocus and get excited about what we could do, rather than wasting my time being disappointed by what we couldn't do.

REVIEW
Run-down buildings

1. **Recognize that something needs attention.**
   Buildings that are in poor shape often mean that some part of you is being neglected. You probably won't have to think too hard about it. You know if you have been feeling down or upset about something, or if you have been letting yourself go physically. The symbolism is there to call your attention to it and let you know that it is time to get things back into shape. If, however, the building is in such bad shape as to be beyond repair, then consider that you may need to let go of something. Perhaps the relationship you are in is never going to be what you need, or your job will never have the potential that you feel that you deserve.

2. **What kind of building are you in?**
   The kind of building you are in will always give you a clue. An office building probably is about work. Bank is most likely about your financial situation. Your home is about your body or personal issues. In my example, the hotels were something that represented the vacations that I was having trouble planning for.

CHAPTER 27

Visual metaphors

Are you alive or are you dead?
Listen to blue
And see what I've said

Figures of speech, phrases, and compound words frequently show up in dreams as odd images. If you are able to read their meaning, they often can show you the root of what the dream is really about.

> *I am walking on a road. The road has rocks in the pavement. I think about how they lay down gravel on the road after they pave it. It is like that, except that the rocks are bigger. I am by a crossroad. That street is smooth. I can see where the rocky road merges into the smooth road. It isn't a noticeable spot where one ends and one begins, but rather more of a slow transition, with some areas becoming smooth earlier than others. I think about how when the road is first paved and the rocks are laid down, it is bumpy, but that it smoothes out over time.*

My divorce caused my life to go through substantial changes on many levels. It affected how often I saw my kids, where I lived, how much money I had, and who I spent my time with. It was hard, but over time I met new friends, adjusted to my schedule, found ways to cope with hard times, and found new things that I enjoyed doing. This dream is full of metaphors, such as "bumpy road" and "crossroads." It refers to a "slow transition" with some areas becoming smooth quicker than others, and that it is bumpy at first but will smooth out over time. This dream had a simple message: Things will smooth out over time.

If you see two or more objects together in a dream that you normally would not associate together, it could be that the dream is trying to "show" you a compound word or euphemism.

> *I am walking down a large flight of stairs. I have my hand on the railing. There is a fluorescent light right underneath the railing and is stretches the full distance of the railing.*

A handrail and fluorescent lights are not something that I have ever seen together like that. Rather than writing it off as odd, I considered names of these objects: *handrail, fluorescent lights.* I considered various other ways to say these words, such as shortening them to *rail* and *light.* After some thought it just clicked with me. My wife and I had a conversation in the car the day before. One of the topics we discussed was about how the state had been looking into putting in a light rail system by a highway near where we live. My dream was trying to get me to see the words *light rail.* The dream wasn't actually about my thoughts on the subject of light rail, but rather it made me think about my conversation with my wife. As I thought about that conversation, I recalled that there was something that my wife had mentioned that caused me to feel a bit of discomfort. It wasn't anything major enough that I even said anything, but dreams have a tendency to bring up small things that you consciously discard. The fact that I didn't allow myself to consciously process something that had bothered me——even a little——caused it to show up in my dream to process it then.

REVIEW
Visual metaphors

1. **Look for clichés.**
   After writing out your dream, look for figures of speech and highlight them. Words such as *crossroads* and *rocky road* in my example made it easier for me to determine the meaning of the dream. My association with those terms is that I am at a place of change and things will be difficult for a while.
2. **Think closely about objects that don't belong together.**
   When objects are put together that normally have nothing to do with each other, your dream may be trying to make a compound word or phrase. Try brainstorming different names for the objects in question. In my example, reducing the name to something more basic gave me my answer. *Handrail* became *rail,* and *fluorescent light* became *light.*

CHAPTER 28

Music in the morning

Turn the dial just a bit
A slight change of frequency makes it all clear

There is an odd method that I sometimes use to help guide me toward the true subject matter of a dream. This same method is also effective in helping me recall my dreams upon awakening, or later in the day. I don't know how many people have music running through their heads when they wake up in the morning, but I'd guess that I'm not the only one. This doesn't occur every day, but it is very frequent. Sometimes the music is instrumental, but more often than not there are lyrics. On occasion the music is something that I had never heard before, but most often I am familiar with the song.

I realized some years ago that the music that runs through my head upon awakening is not random. I began noticing this when the lyrics to the song running through my mind would remind me of something in my dream, prompting my memory of the dream. Sometimes the emotion of the song would match the emotion in my dream. However, most of the time what I have found is that there is some segment of the song lyrics that had showed up in the dream in much the same way that figures of speech and metaphors appear, often visually.

In the following example, I had awakened with a segment of lyrics from the song "High Enough" from *Damn Yankees* running through my head:

"Can you take me high enough, to fly me over yesterday?"

These song lyrics prompted me to recall the following dream:

I am on a bike riding in the backyard of my early childhood home. The bike takes off into the air and flies over two fences. My stomach feels like it would if I were on a roller coaster. I am very high up and I'm afraid it will hurt when I hit the ground. It doesn't hurt, but I do feel the impact. I take off again and fly over one fence this time.

The evening before I had a mediation appointment with my ex-wife to try and divide up our remaining property. There wasn't much that I wanted, but I did ask for a few things that had sentimental value to me. One of those items was a tagalong bike that I had for my son. It attached to the back of my bike so that we could go on rides together. My ex-wife contested this particular item. We ended up spending most of the session trying to resolve just this one item, and we left without an agreement.

In the dream, I am flying over fences on a bike. Based upon the emotional evening prior to this dream in which a tagalong bike was at the center of an argument, the bike symbolism is easy to see. I already know that fences in my dreams represent boundaries. You may also notice that there are two fences that I jump over first, then one more. This is the two-plus-one equation that frequently shows up in my dreams representing my twin daughters and my son. At this point, I have the basic symbolism to tell me the subject matter of the dream.

The feeling in my stomach reminded me of how I felt in mediation. I was tired of the emotional roller coaster. I noticed how, in the dream, I was worried that I would be hurt when I hit the ground. It didn't hurt, but I did feel the impact. After my mediation session, I had been considering that much of this was just not worth it. Even though I didn't want to let go of some things, the stress was not worth it. Still, I had a lot of feelings about walking away from things that meant something to me.

As I was falling asleep the night of this dream, I had been thinking that I might need to rethink the types of memories that I had with my children. In many ways I was best off focusing on the memories that I had created with them since my separation from my ex-wife, rather than trying to hang on to old memories. In my dream I was flying over boundaries. I was afraid that I would get hurt. I did feel the impact, but I didn't get hurt. The song lyrics "fly me over yesterday" not only helped me to remember this dream, but to understand what it was trying to say. Indeed I did need to let some things go. I would feel it, but I'd be okay.

Even if I don't remember a dream, a song running through my head upon awakening can still have an impact on me. Two mornings prior to the previous example, I awoke with some lyrics from the song "Blood Money" by Jon Bon Jovi:

"This ain't about me, and it ain't about you, or the good and the bad times we've both been through."

Even though the song didn't cause me to recall a dream, I understood where the lyrics were coming from. A few weeks earlier I had a previous mediation session with my ex-wife. At one point in the session, I got upset at an accusation against me. I said, "This isn't about me." The mediator interrupted and said, "This isn't about either of you. It is about your children." With my next mediation session just a couple of days away, these lyrics—and I'm sure the dream that I didn't recall—were reminding me of what was most important.

Every so often I will realize that I have music running through my mind before I fall asleep at night. This is different from the music in the morning. The night music is more like the images that I see as I fall asleep. Just as we have predream images, we can also have predream sounds. It may be worth comparing the music that runs through your mind at night with the dreams of that same night. You may find a connection.

REVIEW
Music in the morning

1. **See if the lyrics help you recall a dream.**
   I am convinced that one of the main reasons that I have a song running through my head upon awakening is that it is a system that my mind has used to help me recall my dreams. Usually it isn't the entire song, but some phrase of the song that I "hear" over and over. If you wake up not remembering any dreams but you have music running through your head, lie still for a few minutes and "listen" to the music. Maybe, like me, you can use this tool to help you remember more dreams.

2. **Feel the emotion of the song.**
   Music often provokes an emotion. Certain songs remind you of times from your past. If the song that is running through your head spurs a strong emotion in you, make it a point to write down anything that you can remember from your dreams. Consider this: Thoughts (including music running through your head) come from someplace. So where was your mind just before awakening? Whatever you were dreaming about is what caused that song to be running through your head.

CHAPTER 29

Dream thoughts

Come soar through the night
And share my delight
We'll use my wings
For our lucid flight

Let's walk through this door
Through the years many more
We'll fly to the sky
And together explore

We'll sit by the sea
And watch eternity
These thoughts we have now
Forever shall be

And though we'll wake
Away from the lake
Another dream
I promise to make

So far we have looked into interpreting dreams though actions and symbols. Just as important, or perhaps even more so, are the thoughts that you have in your dreams. Your dream thoughts should match up very closely to something you have been thinking about during your waking hours. In a way, thinking is just another form of action. The difference between your dream thoughts and a dream action is that you are only thinking about something rather than actually doing it. The process of thought is the action. Consider how that relates to your waking life.

I am in my former in-laws' living room with my ex-wife and her parents. I am intending to break it off with my ex-wife, as though I hadn't yet done that. Her father seems aware of what I am about to do, although he says nothing. I realize that I have lived this experience before. It is as though I went back in time and am living this experience again, except that I have knowledge of how everything turns out. I am doing everything exactly the same way that it was done before—what I said, how I moved my body, etc. I think, "I wonder if I can do things differently?" I intentionally move in different ways and say different things. I find out that I can do things differently. So I intend to handle things better with the knowledge that I have.

At this time in my life, I had been starting to change the ways that I was dealing with my ex-wife. We had been arguing and generally getting along poorly for more than two years since our separation. I was beginning to understand that nothing was going to change unless I did things differently. It didn't matter whether or not I believed that I was right. The fact is that we argued virtually every time that we spoke. So I decided that communication between us should be limited to what was absolutely necessary. I also felt that using e-mail made more sense than phone conversations in order to avoid confrontations.

In my dream, I was given a second chance to do things differently. I didn't know what I should do, but I knew that I didn't have to do things the same way that I had been. It was worth experimenting. There was some physical action here. The dream symbolism was that I realized that I could move in different ways or say different things. But it all started with the thought "I wonder if I can do things differently?" Clearly this dream was encouraging me to give that thought a try.

The next time that you write down a dream, include as much as you can about your thoughts. Did you just do some action without thought, or did you make a choice prior to the action? If you act without thinking in your dream, I'd bet that you do the same in real life. On the other hand, you may give way too much thought before acting and miss out on opportunities.

Pay attention to what your thoughts are as you view your dream imagery. After the fact we describe all kinds of weird things ranging from strange-looking people to scary symbolisms. If you do see a strange-looking person, are you really shocked or do you just find it a bit odd? If you are dressed inappropriately, are you self-conscious or doesn't it bother you that much? Where dreams are concerned, it really is the thought that counts. The actions and visual symbols matter only to the extent that you feel something.

REVIEW
Dream thoughts

1. **Do you recall any specific thoughts in your dream?**
    You may not often recall specifically what you were thinking in a dream.
    Most of the time, I recall what I was doing and what the scenery was
    like. But on occasion I can actually remember a thought. If you do, write
    it down and highlight it. Although the situation in your dream may be
    different than waking life, the thought should match up with something
    real. In my example, the thought "I wonder if I can do things differently"
    was easy to match up.

2. **Realize that thoughts are actions.**
    The only difference between thinking about something and physically
    doing something is that in one case you are in the process and in the other
    it has yet to happen. When something has yet to happen, that leaves open
    possibilities. There may be more than one way to do something. In one
    case you may be fixing something and in the other you are thinking that
    something needs to be fixed. There could be many different ways to fix
    whatever is broken, and you need to sort through your alternatives.

CHAPTER 30

The other side of an argument

A fight must have an enemy
And fight they will to combat against thee
'Tis better to spread peace instead
For the battle won't matter when both we are dead

I never cease to be amazed by what I can learn from my dreams. One very common occurrence that I have noticed is that dreams will help me to see things from different perspectives. Generally I have seen this in the form of dreams showing me different options to solve problems.

On occasion, you may have a dream that helps you to see the other side of an argument. Some issues seem very black-and-white to us, such as political issues. Most people either agree with abortion or not. They agree with capital punishment or not. They agree with prayer in schools or not. The following example looks at an issue that I would previously have sworn that my opinion about could not have been budged.

> *I am on a military ship speaking to someone who appears to be*
> *high-ranking. I overhear some of the crew talking about gays in the*
> *military. I voice my opinion to this man on the subject. I state that I*
> *think it is ridiculous not to allow anyone to voluntarily serve his or*
> *her country and that this is nothing more than government-sponsored*
> *discrimination. This man responds to me without getting defensive. He*
> *tells me that it isn't really about whether or not someone is gay. It is*
> *about respecting the uniform. I ask him what he means by that. He*
> *says that the military is loaded with rules, many of which the people*
> *who serve would not agree with. However, the military is reliant on*
> *its members following orders and rules without question, whether or*

*not they agree with it. The people who serve all have to make personal
sacrifices and follow those rules without questioning authority. Many of
these rules are in place for no other reason than to weed out people, and
keep those who can follow the rules without questioning them.*

I have to admit that my opinion on the subject hasn't changed. I still
believe that this form of discrimination should be abolished, and I don't think
the military is acting in its own best interests when denying someone the
right to serve. I also have to admit that, for the first time, I at least saw a side of
the argument that I had never considered. I do see some validity to what the
officer in my dream was telling me. In a military setting, I agree that rules and
structure are vital. Perhaps this is why I wasn't cut out for military life.

Of course the reality of this dream was not to get me to change my mind
about my position on gays in the military. The real purpose was to get me to
deal with other people in a different way. The fact is that I'm not going to be
able to convince other people to see things my way. The point of this dream
was to assist me with communication skills that will be more effective for me.
What I most got out of this dream is that I should first try to understand the
other side of an argument, even if I still don't agree with it. There is value
in understanding even if you still disagree. That value is that you can now
understand that the other person is, in their mind, doing what they believe
is right. If I continue to argue without ever trying to understand the other
side of an argument, I'm setting myself up for a lifetime of frustration. In
the end, I didn't change my mind one bit about my position, but I was able
to nonetheless have a conversation in which both parties felt heard. Many
arguments can be defused simply by first choosing to understand the other
person's position, whether you agree with it or not. It is nothing short of
common courtesy, and that is something we all appreciate. I have many friends
with differing political positions than I have. Friendship has little to do with it.
When the arguing stops, you'll find that you have more common ground than
you had previously realized.

REVIEW
The other side of an argument

1. **Watch for dreams about something that you have a strong
   opinion on.**
   It is so interesting that your dreams will show you gray areas between
   the black-and-white. When you have a dream about something you
   feel strongly about, I bet your dream is trying to show you angles or
   perspectives that you have been unwilling to look at in your daily life.
   What I have learned from these experiences is quite simple. The best
   way to expand your views is to talk less and listen more. In my dream

example I did not interrupt the officer after voicing my opinion. I let him speak.

2. **Pay attention to what the supporting cast is doing.**

    In my example, the supporting cast were crew members who were getting me angry over their opinion. This was the setup. It brought out the emotion of anger, and opinion, over a specific issue.

CHAPTER 31

Knowing

What were your last thoughts?
Did you believe in fate?
Did you learn to love or did you harbor hate?

Did you live in the moment?
Or did you lay down a goal?
Does heaven now hold your eternal soul?

Had you been just a child?
Or did you have your first kiss?
Of what on this Earth is it most that you'll miss?

Were you happy with the way that you lived your days?
Or were you sad and afraid?
Will the separateness, once fused, slowly fade?

Is it okay to feel sad for your sudden end?
Or shall I simply feel grateful you were?
Am I correct to know that the heart you carried was so very pure?

Did you see with the eyes of spirit?
Did they give you wings for your flight?
If I look into the nighttime sky, will I know which one is your light?

No matter how much you read about dream interpretations and premonitions, ultimately you have to experience precognition for yourself in order to fully believe in it. As I mentioned at the beginning of this book, you will know it when you nail a dream interpretation. If you "think" that you got it right, you are missing something. When you know it, there's no question. The same can hold true for premonition dreams. When something from a dream shows up in real life, I instantly have this feeling of "Now I know what that dream was about!" Still, when it comes to premonitions even the most open-minded of us carry a healthy dose of skepticism. What ultimately got me to believe—to know—was the fact that there simply were too many things that I could not explain. Although this knowing came from many dreams over a long period of time, I recall the dream in which any remaining doubt was removed.

> *I am in a plain white room that has no furniture except a white restaurant booth. There is a door, but I see only the knob. My wife and her ex-husband are shaking the doorknob until a fluid comes out of it. They put this fluid into a syringe and inject it into themselves. The scene moves into a bathroom, which is also very white. My wife is wearing a low-cut shirt and I see that her chest is very inflamed. The inflammation is in the shape of a heart and covers most of her chest. There is also a smaller area of inflammation on her left upper side closer to her shoulder. She tells me about how she and her ex-husband had injected this fluid from the doorknob and it made her sick. She is very upset and afraid, and she says that she feels like she's going to die. The amount of inflammation that I see concerns me, but I don't believe that she is going to die. The scene now looks the same but feels like it is a bit later. I see that almost all of the inflammation on her chest is gone. There is just a little bit remaining on her upper left side.*

My wife and I went to the mall later in the same day that I had this dream. While we were on an escalator, my wife out of nowhere stopped speaking, a blank stare on her face. I asked her what was wrong and she said that she had a flashback—a memory. She remembered something hurtful from her former marriage. I asked her what made her recall it at that particular moment, but she had no explanation. I told her about my dream at this point, having found it a bit odd that her ex-husband happened to show up in my dream this same day. The following evening we went out for a late Valentine's dinner. We didn't have the opportunity to go on Valentine's Day, so we made a date on the Friday night following—which, as it turned out, was the anniversary of my wife's divorce. My wife went to use the restroom at the restaurant, and someone had gotten sick in there. With that exception, it was a nice evening. The following afternoon my wife began not feeling well, and by morning she had a fever and flu symptoms. After another couple of days I took her to the doctor and they confirmed her positive for influenza, despite her having had a flu shot. By the next day she began having trouble breathing. I again took her to the doctor and this time they also found pneumonia. She was given medication for it, yet continued to get worse through the night. I decided to take her to the emergency room early the following morning, where they determined that her entire left lung was filled. They gave her additional treatments and medication before sending her home. It took a couple of weeks before she was feeling better. Her illness scared me a couple of times, but I also had this knowing that everything was going to be okay. My dream was with me. I clearly remember seeing the inflammation on her in my dream, days before she had even the slightest symptom. During the time that my wife was ill, her mother called and made it a point to let me know that I should wipe down all the doorknobs in the house. As soon as she said this, I remembered the doorknob in my dream. My wife had gotten sick in the dream because of a fluid that came out of a doorknob. Her ex-husband in the dream symbolized the beginning of her ordeal. She had a flashback about him, unexplained, and shortly thereafter got sick. I wondered later if my wife might have gotten sick by touching the doorknob at the restaurant where someone had gotten ill in the ladies' room. While my wife was sick, she was worried that I'd get sick too. I was around her constantly, even sleeping in the same bed. I knew that I wouldn't get sick, because I didn't get sick in the dream. Only my wife was sick in the dream.

Although you can read about my dream, nobody but me can ever actually have experienced it. I know the emotions and gut instincts that go along with the symbols in this dream, and I know this is a true premonition. There is no way that I could have known days in advance that my wife would get ill, much less with inflammation in her chest—even so far as noticing the left side, which is the lung that got filled. The chance that I would have a dream about her getting sick from a doorknob, only to have her mother specifically mention that I should clean the doorknobs, is certainly odd. To add in that I dreamt of my wife's ex-husband being involved in this on the same day that she had an unexplained hurtful memory about him is also strange, especially considering that the Valentine's date occurred on the anniversary of their divorce. And, of course, the inflammation was in the shape of a heart, indicating that this came from Valentine's Day. Obviously I could not have known a day in advance that someone was going to get ill in the ladies room the following night at the restaurant we were going to.

This dream convinced me. I was about ninety percent of the way there anyway, but my doubt ceased to exist after this. This was not some minor coincidence; nor was it something that I could have known even on a subconscious level. I finally accepted that I really do pick up on signals from somewhere.

In the following chapters I will discuss my theories on where these signals come from and why they are a part of our lives. I believe without question that any dream interpretation book that does not include future events as part of the imagery and symbolisms is missing a big piece of the puzzle. I'd go so far as to say that it is impossible to fully interpret a dream without factoring in these future events.

Once you experience this for yourself, you too will find your knowing. Whispers come to us in dreams, but they also come to us in other ways. This book is a whisper. As I write this, I do not know if it is meant for just one other person to see or many others, but I know that it was meant to be written and it is in your hands at this time for a reason.

REVIEW
Knowing

1. **Look for the unexplainable.**
   This begins with writing down your dreams. Unexplained events most often occur within a few days of the dream, so you'll have time to document the dream prior to the event. Consider what you could have known, even at a subconscious level, and what you could not possibly have known. Could I have known that an evacuation affecting my daughter would occur later in the same day that I had a dream with that very title? In this case, no, I could not. Could my stepdaughter have picked up subconsciously that she'd be moving? Yes, she most definitely could have. Just this morning I had a dream in which I overheard my wife stating that she would like to date Kurt Russell. I woke up thinking, "What the hell was that about?" Later that morning my wife and I were watching the morning news show when they had a story on dating, which got us talking a bit about some dates we'd been on prior to meeting each other. Although the conversation was innocent, the thought of my wife dating someone else made me a bit uneasy. No sooner did those feelings pop into my head than the morning news anchor said that following the commercial they were going to show a recent interview with Kurt Russell. I know that most people would say, "That's an interesting coincidence," or even just laugh this off. But for me, this happens so darn often that I did find myself chuckle at it, thinking, "Cool. Now I know what this dream was about." The emotions in the dream matched perfectly against my real-life emotions. There was no doubt, and you will know exactly what I'm talking about as you learn to master this skill.
2. **Keep an open mind.**
   There is nothing wrong with being skeptical. Just don't close the door on possibility. The fact is, most people understand very little about their dreams. They spend hours every night in dreams yet remember little, and most don't even consider their meaning or where they came from. My guess is that you do have an open mind, or you wouldn't be reading this book.
3. **Be skeptical too.**
   Along with an open mind, it is good to keep a healthy dose of skepticism as well. Don't force something into being a premonition just because you want to believe it. Most of my dream material is not precognitive. What turns out to be a premonition is not always the part of a dream that I would have expected. Be patient. It will come.

CHAPTER 32

Daytime whispers

A prayer to the morning sun
The shadow and the light are one
And for this new day just begun
Thy bygone sins may be undone

Dreams have an aura of mystery about them. If you carry that same sense of the mystic during waking hours, you will see that whispers show up there too with regularity. It may be a well-timed phone call from a friend you haven't spoken to in months, or the slow car that prevents you from being a part of the accident further up the road. It may be the answer to a question being heard in the song playing on the radio when your alarm goes off in the morning, or the chance encounter with a stranger. I see it all the time, and you too will see that these "coincidences" once again occur too often to be coincidental.

I was out shopping for holiday gifts for my wife. I decided to stop in a bookstore, although I had nothing specific in mind. My wife is half American Indian, so I wandered into that section of the store. An Indian man then walked up to me with a book in his hands. He said to me, "You need to buy this book. It may be for you, or for you to read to your kids, but it needs to be in your home." The man spoke with such passion about this book, which was a series of Native American short stories about such things as wisdom and bravery. At one time I may have dismissed this as a crazy stranger bugging me in the store, but by this time I was seeing the world through different eyes. I bought the book and gave it to my wife. We read through the stories in this book together, which made the stories all the more enjoyable. The man was right. This book did belong in my home.

My wife and I had been out looking at garage sales. I'd had neck surgery a week before and it was the first time I had been able to get out of the house for a few hours, albeit with a neck brace. It turned out to be a rainy day, so all of the sales were literally held inside of the garages. Of course I had been questioned a few times during the day what had happened to my neck. Most people assumed that I had been in a car accident, but at one sale a man came up to me and asked me if I'd had disc surgery. I explained to him that I had a C6–C7 discectomy and fusion, which he fully understood. It turned out he had the same problem but had been putting off having surgery for several years, all the while living in pain. He asked how long I was in the hospital and was surprised that it was only one night, with my total recovery period also much less than he thought. As we talked further, it turned out that the doctor he had seen years earlier was the same doctor who did my surgery. By the time we left the sale, the man said that he might call the doctor and set up an appointment. My belief is that this was more than coincidence. I was where I was supposed to be at that moment.

Books seem to be a very common way for whispers to come to me. One day I was at the library and couldn't find anything that looked interesting to me. I was about to leave, when several feet away from where I was standing, I saw a single book standing up on an open part of a shelf. I don't know why, but I walked over and looked at the book. This book was the true story of a blind man who climbs mountains. I've never climbed mountains, but the subject matter interests me. I decided to get the book and it was fantastic. I was very inspired by it. I felt that if a blind man could climb the world's highest mountains, I really had no excuse not to give a bit more effort to the things that I do. It was the right book at the right time for me. As I was reading the book, I recalled the dream that I'd had a year earlier about the blind man being guided up the mountain.

As I am writing this book, I only recently found out that I might not be able to have more children. My wife and I married in our later thirties, so the biological clock has been ticking fast lately. We had various conversations about whether or not we should attempt to have another child, only to find out that I probably cannot. Still, we kicked around some names for the fun of it. The name Maggie seemed to stick as a girl's name. During that time, my wife and I got new cell phones. The dealer we went to turned out to be a crackpot who sold us a used phone for more than we should have paid for a new one. My wife went to another store that handles this particular service to find out why her phone wasn't working, only to find out it was listed to someone else—named Maggie. Then one day I went to the bookstore—the same one that the Indian man showed up at. I was looking at some books from a particular author whose work I've been enjoying lately. His books were on the bottom shelf, but there was a stool on the floor so I was able to squat down and look through them. As I sat there, I heard a book fall off the shelf at the end of the isle, which was strange because I hadn't even touched the shelf. I got up to go put the book back on the shelf. I could see the open spot from which it fell, so I placed it back there. Then I noticed just above this book was another that had a title that caught my attention. This other book was entitled *Maggie's Miracle*. *Maggie* has been showing up all over the place in recent months. I'm not sure if it is literal or figurative, and perhaps it will take months longer to determine that. In any case it feels like more than coincidence when something shows up repeatedly in your life. Within dreams, repetitive symbols are there to guide you in the right direction or to point out a habit or repeating pattern in your life. It isn't so different in waking life.

I could go on and on with these types of examples, enough to fill another book, I'm sure, but I will leave this chapter with just one more example. In two subsequent books that I read lately, I kept on seeing the theme of following a dream to its end and having faith. Along with that, one book several times had the phrase *it is written* in it. I had described to my wife that writing this book to me is as though I'm writing something that is already written. I'm just the instrument to put in down on paper. I keep on getting signs that I am supposed to write this book. I don't know really for whom, but I have this knowing that it is supposed to be written. Whoever has made it this far into the book no doubt was meant to have it. It could also be that it is important for me to finish this book for no other reason than to see something important to me through to the end.

REVIEW
Daytime whispers

1. **Believe that everything has meaning.**
   Look at everything that happens in your life as though there is meaning behind it, and that it is meant to be. By doing so, I believe that very often you will find truth in that. When a stranger talks to you in public, listen to what they are saying. Don't choose to be annoyed or pass judgment on this person. Not only do I believe that many good things will show up in your life, but it is a wonderful way to view the world. By believing that there is meaning in seemingly meaningless events, you will find yourself far less stressed and generally see life as more interesting.

2. **Pay attention to "coincidences."**
   A single event may not convince you that these whispers, or whatever you choose to call them, are true. But after you have noted it down many times, I bet you do believe. Keep in mind that these events may not be just to benefit you. You could end up in a certain place for someone else's benefit, as I believe was the case at the garage sale. Between nighttime and daytime whispers, you will eventually realize that this is a part of life that you've been blind to up until now. The universe is speaking to you. You need only listen.

CHAPTER 33

What are the whispers?

When my leaf falls from the tree
It shall be replaced with another
And then still another
And through the years shall carry on
Until the tree too has come to pass
And then that tree shall plant a seed
For another
And then still another

Answering this question is the most difficult part of writing this book. Everything else that I have written is something that I know about and can explain. I know about dreams. I have a good understanding of their language and symbolisms, including premonitions. I no longer believe in coincidences and I can tell many stories both for myself and other people to help illustrate what this book has been about. But what exactly are these whispers? Why do these so-called coincidences occur? Why do dreams predict future events? The truth be told, I am a long way from having all the answers to those questions, although I hope that through my dreams I will learn more along the way. The best I can do at this point is put together some things based on the knowledge that I do have.

One thing I know for sure is that these dream premonitions and daytime "coincidences" are real. I have seen far too much to believe otherwise. I also believe that, with practice, you will know this on your own without having to determine if my dream examples are real or not. In fact, that is my goal for this book. I want people to be able to experience this for themselves, rather than believing based only on what they've read or heard about in this book or from other sources. Maybe by now you have had that experience or perhaps you will shortly. Once you do, I suspect that you will start asking yourself the same question that I have been asking. What is this?

One possibility is that there is a scientific explanation. Scientists already know that time is not as it seems. If ever you have the opportunity to read about Einstein's theory of relativity, I suggest you do so. We as humans have learned much about the universe, but there is also so much we don't know. We can't see electricity, but we know it exists. Signals come into our televisions, radios, and cell phones everyday and we don't question it. Perhaps what I have been picking up on is something like a radio signal. Maybe someday this will be just as explainable as electricity or radio waves.

Although I believe that the day could come when much of this can be scientifically explained, I also believe that there is more to it than just some random signals that I pick up on. I will openly admit that I very much would like to believe that there is more. Life has more meaning when everything seems to have a purpose. But as much as I'd like to believe that, it still has to make sense to me. The main reason that I believe that it is not random is that I have picked up on things that have been helpful to me at the right time and place. Random signals wouldn't do that. As an example, the dream that I had about my wife's inflammation in her chest was very helpful to me. I was very worried about her, as well I should have been, but the dream let me know that everything was going to be okay.

I mentioned earlier that full interpretation of a dream involves not only an event that just happened within the last couple of days, but also events that will happen in the next couple of days. It is as though "now" in dreamtime runs approximately from a few days before the dream until a few days after the dream. What you dream about is related to how you are currently feeling, even if the roots of that feeling are from years earlier. But what you are feeling may occur the next day, or the day after. Perhaps the best that I really have to offer here is to say that I get that same "I nailed it" feeling that I get when I properly interpret a dream. I just know, somehow, that these whispers were meant for me specifically. I see them as signposts that tell me that I am exactly where I am supposed to be. They have never failed me. If I listen to these whispers, everything always turns out well. If they were random, then I would have to believe that the results would also be random.

My current working theory on the predictive nature of dreams in based on the space and time we occupy while in those dreams. It hit me one day when my wife made a suggestion to me after reading a rough draft of this book. She noticed that in my evacuation dream, the building was curved so that while looking out of the windows I could still see the building. Her thought was that the school to which the evacuated students were taken was, in real life, curved. If you keep walking through the main hallway, eventually you will end up back where you started. I found this to be an interesting observation and realized that there must in fact be some reason, as with everything in dreams, that the building was curved. Something wasn't quite clicking with me about the school itself, but her suggestion did cause another idea to come into my head as I recalled the dream. I was not only facing the building, but I was up one flight and somewhat to the left of the window that I was looking into. As I was mentally reliving this dream, I had the feeling that this is all about angles, or perspective. I recalled many other dreams in which I specifically took notice of my angles and perspective, such as my black-and-white movie dreams. In those dreams, I was always looking at the screen from some angle, and I knew that those dreams were teaching me to see much more than the obvious in my dreams. Suddenly it all made sense to me. The angles are how I am looking through space and time. I am not just seeing forward, backward, up, down, left, and right. I am seeing three-dimensional angles. Could it be that by paying attention to the dimensions inside of a dream, and where things appear in respect to where you are that future events can be pinpointed? My dream had the school wrap around so that it is both where I am currently standing and also in front of me. Dreams are all about the metaphor. I am seeing something ahead of me that is in the same place where I currently stand.

As far as what the whispers themselves are, I really don't know—at least not yet. I don't know if it is God (or whatever name you choose), spirits of deceased relatives and friends, guides, energy, or a higher form of myself that lives in the spirit world. Whatever they are, they seem familiar and friendly. They communicate with me how they can, either through dreams or by placing people or events in the right places for me to see them. They give me hope that there is more beyond this life, and more within this life. They make my life better, they help me through difficult times, and I have this feeling that I'm being guided toward some destiny that I am to fulfill—perhaps this book, perhaps more.

REVIEW
What are the whispers?

1. **Know for yourself.**
   In the end, everything that I have said in this entire book is meaningless until you experience what I have said for yourself. You will know it when you get a dream properly interpreted. You will know it when you dreamt of something in advance that you could not possibly have otherwise known about. And you will know that the whispers are there to help you.
2. **Try looking at the world through different filters.**
   If your world is perfect just the way that it is, then there is no reason to try anything new. But if you feel that you would like more in your life, then why not try to explore? Even if you aren't sure whether or not you

can believe in it just yet, if the way that you are currently living isn't fully working for you, then why not try something else? You have nothing to lose and everything to gain. Try experimenting with believing, or least with having an open mind.

3. **It's all about the angle.**

Pay very close attention to what angles you are looking at in a dream, particularly if the angle is not just up, down, left, right, etc. If the angle seems to cut diagonally across the dream, I believe that you will find more interesting daytime experiences that follow.

Awakening

Go to sleep
…Dream

Dream of buying a book
It will help you see your past, present, and future

You will learn to understand how everything is connected
And how to be at peace with yourself and the world

It is your choice to use this knowledge
And make the world a better place

Others will follow you
And learn from your example

Perhaps this isn't a dream after all
Maybe it is real

Dreams and the waking world really aren't so different. What you think about becomes reality. The only difference is that our experience of time in a dream is different. In a dream, your thought materializes instantly, whereas in waking life it could take days, weeks, months, or years. Either way the end result is the same. Dreams provide us with a way of finding out how it all will turn out without having to wait to see the result.

Perhaps the description of dreams as egotistical is not actually correct, because that implies selfishness. Although they are always about you, I have never heard of a dream that advises someone to cause harm to another person. I think a better way to describe the nature of dreams is that they show you how best to deal with yourself, knowing that any attempt to change people or circumstances outside of your control is fruitless. You aren't going to change another person. It is possible that a change in yourself may spark inspiration in others, but that is their decision to make. Every dream that we have tells us this. It isn't just what we do; it is what we don't do. Pay attention to the choices that you make in your dreams. There is much to learn, and yet the lessons are always so simple.

> *I am walking down an empty street. I see some trees in front of me, of which I take particular notice. One is full with leaves. I suddenly realize that I am dreaming. Nothing strange happens, but I just know. I take off and fly, going higher than the trees. I come back to the ground and see my son. I hold out my hand and he takes it with his, neither of us saying a word. I take of flying again, this time with my son. We fly for a while together. I begin to have some doubts, not about this being a dream but about my ability to fly. I then start to drop and I feel the sensation of dropping in my stomach. I know that it is my thought that causes me to drop, and then I fly free again. I bring my son back to the ground, and then I take back off to fly some more.*

I had insomnia and my mind was wandering. Being up during the middle of the night can be a strange experience. It is so dark and quiet, and your thoughts go places that they don't have time to go during the day. I thought about spiritual experiences and wondered if I might have one during this sleepless night. Indeed I did in the form of this lucid dream example. While I had been thinking of spiritual experiences, I wished for a dream that would tell me how real my whispers are. What I found in this dream is something that I already knew, but enjoyed being reminded of. I needed to eliminate doubt. Without doubt, I could fly. With doubt, I dropped and felt it in my stomach. I literally do get stomach issues with stress. I played the role of both the father and the son. There is peace in believing.

Trust your dreams. They are your guides. They are your wisdom. They are the highest version of who you are and who you can become.

Sweet dreams.

BIBLIOGRAPHY

Calabrese, Adrian. *Sacred Signs: Hear, See & Believe Messages from the Universe.* Woodbury, MN: Llewellyn Publications, 2006

Coelho, Paulo. *The Alchemist.* New York, NY: HarperSanFrancisco, 2005

_____. *The Zahir: A Novel of Obsession.* New York, NY: HarperCollins, 2005

Dyer, Wayne. *Inspiration: Your Ultimate Calling.* Carlsbad, CA: Hay House, Inc., 2006

_____. *There's a Spiritual Solution to Every Problem.* New York, NY: HarperCollins, 2001

_____. *Wisdom of the Ages.* New York, NY: HarperCollins, 1998

Gongloff, Robert P. *Dream Exploration: A New Approach.* Woodbury, MN: Llewellyn Publications, 2006

Kharitidi, Olga. *Entering the Circle: Ancient Secrets of Siberian Wisdom Discovered by a Russian Psychiatrist.* New York, NY: HarperSanFrancisco, 1996

Kingsbury, Karen. *Maggie's Miracle.* Brentwood, TN: Warner Books, 2003

LaBerge, Stephen and Howard Rheingold. *Exploring the World of Lucid Dreaming.* New York, NY: Ballatine Books, 1991

Longfellow, Henry Wadsworth. *Selected Poems.* New York, NY: Penguin Books, 1988

Marshall, Joseph M. III. *The Lakota Way: Stories and Lessons for Living.* New York, NY: Penguin Putman, Inc., 2002

Moss, Robert. *Dreamgates*. New York, NY: Three Rivers Press, 1998

Radha, Swami Sivananda. *Realities of the Dreaming Mind*. Spokane, WA: Timeless Books, 1994

Seeds, Michael A. *Horizons: Exploring the Universe*. Belmont, CA: Wadsworth Publishing Company, 1995

Sagan, Carl. *Cosmos*. New York, NY: Ballatine Books, 1980

Stepanek, Mattie J.T. *Reflections of a Peacemaker: A Portrait Through Heartsongs*. Kansas City, MO: McMeel Publishing, 2005

Weihenmayer, Erik. *Touch the Top of the World: A Blind Man's Journey to Climb Farther Than the Eye Can See*. New York, NY: Penguin Putnam, Inc., 2001

Wolfson, Richard. *Simply Einstein: Relativity Demystified*. New York, NY. W.W. Norton & Company, Inc., 2003

COSIMO is a specialty publisher of books and publications that inspire, inform, and engage readers. Our mission is to offer unique books to niche audiences around the world.

COSIMO BOOKS publishes books and publications for innovative authors, nonprofit organizations, and businesses. COSIMO BOOKS specializes in bringing books back into print, publishing new books quickly and effectively, and making these publications available to readers around the world.

COSIMO CLASSICS offers a collection of distinctive titles by the great authors and thinkers throughout the ages. At COSIMO CLASSICS timeless works find new life as affordable books, covering a variety of subjects including: Business, Economics, History, Personal Development, Philosophy, Religion & Spirituality, and much more!

COSIMO REPORTS publishes public reports that affect your world, from global trends to the economy, and from health to geopolitics.

Printed in the United States
81007LV00002B/103-156

9 781602 067172